Black Media in Minnesota
Tradition, Practice, & Vision

Contributors

Henry Banks, Donnie Nicole Belcher, Daniel Pierce Bergin
Dr. Danielle K. Brown, Georgia Fort, Dr. Robin P. Hickman-Winfield, Lissa Jones-Lofgren, Al McFarlane, Jasmine Snow
Dr. Catherine R. Squires, Dallas Watson
Tracey Williams-Dillard & Dr. Mahmoud El-Kati

Published by In Black Ink • inblackink.org

Black Media in Minnesota

Tradition, Practice, & Vision

Edited by
Al McFarlane

Foreword by
Dr. Mahmoud El-Kati

Contributors
Donnie Nicole Belcher, Daniel Pierce Bergin
Dr. Danielle K. Brown, Georgia Fort
Dr. Robin P. Hickman-Winfield, Lissa Jones-Lofgren
Al McFarlane, Jasmine Snow, Dr. Catherine R. Squires
Dallas Watson, & Tracey Williams-Dillard
Henry Banks

In Black Ink

Copyright © 2024 by In Black Ink
First Printing
Printed in the United States of America

Black Media in Minnesota: Tradition, Practice, & Vision
Edited by Al McFarlane

ISBN: 979-8-9895065-3-8

Summary
Thirteen media makers from Minnesota discuss the issues, importance, challenges, and history of media, in particular Black media, and its impact on community.

Contributor's Essay Copyrights

Banks, Henry. "Duluth, Minnesota, at a Crossroads: Solutions for Becoming a Beloved Community of the North."

Belcher, Donnie Nicole. "Hear the Children."

Bergin, Daniel Pierce. "How Publisher Cecil Newman Made His Mark on the Minnesota Newspaper Industry."

Bergin, Daniel Pierce. "Listening for Black Voices."

Brown, Danielle K. "Sticks, Stones, and Words that Hurt: Considering the Revolution Within."

El-Kati, Mahmoud. "Foreword: The Historical Impact of American Media on People of African Descent."

Fort, Georgia. "Credibility of the Source: How Journalistic Bias Is Slowing Social Progress."

Hickman-Winfield, Robin P. "Walking in the Footsteps of Uncle Gordon: Keeping the Promise."

Jones-Lofgren, Lissa. "Reclaiming My Historical Imagination."

McFarlane, Al. "Authoring a Future in Which We Win."

McFarlane, Al. "A Case Study: Frederick Douglass—Literacy and Creating a Voice for His People."

Snow, Jasmine. "Storytelling - More than a Defense Mechanism."

Squires, Catherine R. "Black Media and Censorship: A Brief History of White Supremacist 'Cancel Culture.'"

Watson, Dallas. "Black Media."

Williams-Dillard, Tracey. "*Minnesota Spokesman-Recorder*: A Family Legacy."

Professional Services
Editing: Danielle Magnuson
Development Team: Uri-Biia H. Si-Asar & Micah Roetman
Desktop Publishing & Graphic Design: Papyrus Publishing Inc.

This publication was produced for educational purposes.

All rights reserved. International copyright secured. No part of this book may be reproduced, stored in a retrieval system, or transmitted in any form or by any means, whether electronic, mechanical, photocopying, recording or otherwise, without prior written permission of the publisher, except for inclusion of brief quotations in an acknowledged review.

In Black Ink
938 Selby Avenue
St. Paul, Minnesota 55104
info@inblackink.org

In Black Ink (IBI) is a nonprofit organization that creates spaces where the intergenerational stories about Minnesotans of African Heritage can be shared, documented, and archived. In Black Ink provides publishing arts initiatives and opportunities to communities that have been disenfranchised historically and continue to be presently. IBI's cultural literacy programming mitigates the damage of economic, educational, and cultural inequities that are the result of past and current prejudice and discrimination.

We are grateful to the Minnesota State Arts Board and the Metropolitan Regional Arts Council funders for their generous support of artists and the arts.

A Sankofa Series Publication

Acknowledgments

Who we are often tends to be who others tell us we are in the reflections of their stories of us. The Sankofa Event & Series was started to help shift the narrative and elevate the voice of those who lived the experience, often talked about by others who simply observed them. Much appreciation and great thanks to our vibrant Minnesota Black media makers, journalists, storytellers, and narrative change agents. Your bravery in shifting the focus to elevate the voice of the community provides us with a future conceived and nurtured by us.

In Black Ink

Foreword

The Historical Impact of American Media on People of African Descent

This wonderful publication produced in conjunction with the Sankofa Event & Series is a testament to the collective will and work of African people. This is the third publication to take on this unique aspect of addressing community issues with local Minnesotan expert voices. The Sankofa Event & Series attempts to inspire change through engaging discussion and reflection. In Black Ink organizes this annual event and provides support for the corresponding publication for that year. This anthology brings together twelve of our brightest local scholars, activists, media makers, and institution-builders from Minnesota to address one of the most complex issues of our time. This issue of Black people and the media is worthy of our attention, discussion, and reflection. It is to our great benefit that these contributors will guide us through their thoughts on this issue.

The "white"[1] press has monopolized what has been their total power to define Black people in a thousand different ways, all of which offer no redeeming value that makes us human. These articles provide a place for people to see the world through the eyes of Black people, who have different lenses. These lenses provide a perspective not often represented in mainstream American media, one of self-respect and self-definition, that allows the Black community to answer the questions "Who am I?" "Where did I come from?" "Where am I going?" The goal is for Black people to get out of this oppressive system by taking a note from the Old Testament story of Job and defining our humanity through rebellion and resolve.

The Black Press did a good job of countering the negative image that the white press was making of us. Our churches had organs, literary clubs, and other smaller community clubs that served as vehicles to help ward off those images provided through written commentary and visual imagery. Our response to the white supremacist newspapers was the Black Press and the Black news media outlets.

The historical impact of American media on people of African descent is enormous. It has helped shape what we know as "the race problem" or "the Negro problem" in the United States. Black people's narrative has long been in the hands of the media. What do I mean when I say "media"? Media is a plural word that means all forms of mass communication—for example radio, newspapers, theater, television, and online social media. Each is a medium. Another word for media was given to us by C. Wright Mills who wrote a book in 1956 titled *The Power Elite*. He coined the term "cultural apparatus" which determines American culture through mass media and how it is exposed, expressed, and established as an institution. Media has been around since the "town crier," who would inform the public verbally on behalf of an institution or official body. What media does is send messages, images, and symbols to the populace as to what society is, who is there, who is a hero, and who is not. It deals with the whole spectrum of life.

Black people and media go back to the dawn of American history. It begins with newspapers, the first great medium of mass media. The newspaper has been called the "first draft of history." Modern media shapes the popular opinion of the masses of people. In the United States at the very beginning, America's first continuously published newspaper, *The Boston News-Letter*, published its first issue in 1704. America's first independent newspaper, *The New-England Courant*, was published by Benjamin Franklin's older brother in 1721. By the start of the Revolutionary War in 1775, there were thirty-seven independent US newspapers to keep the public informed. The nation's first daily newspaper, *The Pennsylvania Packet* and *Daily Advertiser*, began publication in 1784. *The New York Post*, established in 1801, is the nation's oldest continuously published daily newspaper. As one can imagine, during the time of African enslavement, American media was very harsh in its description and representation of the Black/African descendent community. The media instituted the very ideal of African people living in a caste system, of being chattel, and being inferior beings. The majority of the messages coming from this medium were dehumanizing toward African people.

An example of a newspaper shaping mass opinion is *The New York Times*, which is a mass media institution that distributes its newspaper over the entire country. Also, the *Times* is emblematic of the American newsprint media. In my opinion, it has been one of the more effective mediums, up until radio and television, in painting stereotypes of Black people as clowns, buffoons, ignoramuses, and the like. It is not simply a national newspaper, but an international one that has played a significant role in the dehumanization of Black people's image and likeness in popular media across the globe. The *Times* and other news outlets promoted lynching due to their deracination of Black people in print by making them appear to be like animals, like criminals, and violent in the white public eye. The *Times* and others simply projected blatant racist news coverage of the entire Black community for hundreds of years. Recently these historically "white" newspapers have begun to apologize for their role in the making of racist America. See more from Brent Staples in his article "How the White Press Wrote Off Black America," published in the *Times*.

There was a counternarrative produced by the abolitionists that defended the humanity and rights of African people at that time. The abolitionists would paint Black people as beings to be pitied, empathized with, and humanized. Some examples of abolitionist newspapers were *The Liberator*, published by William Lloyd Garrison, and *The North Star*, published by Frederick Douglass, a formerly enslaved African, who had one of the most effective mediums in America in exalting the humanity of African people. Again, for the most part, newspapers during the antebellum period made the greatest contribution to dehumanizing and vilifying Black people and making Black people invisible in the eyes of the country and the world. The term used to describe such an insidious process on a people is *social death*. Social death means that one is not a part of society and might as well be dead in all aspects of life except the exploitative aspects of one's labor. Social death is equivalent to being not human, being a living tool, or "a species of property," as George Washington, the father of this country, put it. So social death means that you don't exist as a human being and, to the extent you do exist, you exist as a stereotype: despised, ignorant, happy-go-lucky, violent, criminal, or entertainer. Most newspapers in the years coming out of slavery, with very few exceptions, imaged Black people as clowns, buffoons and deformed inferior humans.

Another medium is entertainment, including live performances. American theater started on the "slave" plantation, with enslaved Africans entertaining themselves and the "masters." African people sang, danced, and performed comedy for themselves, and the owners appropriated those forms for their entertainment. Early American entertainment came with "white" people obscenely imitating African people's customs and cultural forms for their pleasure. This was a type of acculturation or culture colonization, and it was integrated into the collective "white" psyche of the time. By the turn of the 1800s, Black Face minstrels had taken hold and were in full bloom across the entire country. This derogatory art form was comprised of "white" men taking the entertainment cultural practice of African people off the plantation, bastardizing it, and putting it on stage for America. Black Face minstrels involved the caricaturing and the malevolent imitation on stage of Black people for "white" people's entertainment. They stereotypically imitated Black people by putting burnt black cork on their faces and red or white makeup on their lips and around their mouths to exaggerate the size of their lips. This extreme caricature of Black people plays out in the "white" psyche today.

Black Face minstrels were dominated by "whites," meaning "white" people grossly imitated Black people for entertainment and money all over the country during the 1800s up until the Civil War. This can be considered one of the earliest acts of cultural appropriation of Black culture and life, although a grotesque one. After the Civil War, due to the colonization of thought or the permeation of white supremacy in the Black mind, newly freed Black people began imitating "white" people who were stereotypically imitating Black people. Thus, Black people would also put burnt black cork on their faces, no matter how dark they already were. Again, they would put red or white makeup on their lips and around their mouth to exaggerate the size of their lips. This sick theatrical practice dominated up until the early 1900s. Black troupes were one of minstrelsy's last bastions, as more white performers moved into vaudeville or performed variety shows with comedy and music that weren't based on "race." However, Black troupes performed scant shows up until the 1960s. I saw one show personally in Florida in 1955. Often these shows were booked and managed by a white-controlled institution called the Theatre Owners Booking Association

(TOBA), although Black performers called this exploitative institution TOBA (Tough on Black Actors) for their many unfair labor practices.

The Black newsprint medium was always our savior. The Black newspaper maintained our humanity, our focus on freedom, and our consciousness as a community. The power and creative role of Black journalism began with the publication of *Freedom's Journal* in 1827, the first Black owned and operated weekly newspaper. The Black newspapers I grew up on were a part of my life. I don't know the world without such newspapers as *The Chicago Defender*, *The Pittsburgh Courier*, or the *Baltimore Afro-American*. It was this way for millions of Black people. I grew up in a world in which that's all that I saw my grandmother read. That's what she used, partially, to teach me to read and educate me—the Black newspapers. Reading and supporting and getting the Black newspaper was a cultural practice for my family; it seemed natural. Many in our younger generations, like those born after the Civil Rights and Black Power movements, don't know of this piece of our cultural fabric. My knowledge of the Black community, culture, history, and the issues we are wrestling with came from these Black newspapers. The knowledge acquired by those who grew up with the Black Press might be equivalent to a high school diploma. It's through this medium that I encountered Joel A. Rodgers, P.L. Prattis, W.E.B. Du Bois, Evelyn Cunningham, and Ethel Payne, the great editorial writers, before I ever stepped onto a college campus. I was raised on the editorial pages of a Black newspaper, which was written by brilliant Black scholars, business leaders, community leaders, and writers. I encountered the Honorable Elijah Muhammad in the editorial section of *The Pittsburgh Courier*. He wrote a column entitled Mr. Muhammad Speaks, which later became the title of the Nation of Islam's national newspaper: *Muhammad Speaks*.

The merits of Black newspapers as a cultural institution can't be overstated. Many of our cultural institutions—such as Black churches, lodges, and fraternal and civic organizations—would make our behavior somewhat predictable. The Black newspaper gave us a different perspective on information and knowledge. They allowed us to develop a different narrative. They encouraged us to speak up against injustices, for example. They helped to shape national voices. It gave Black people similar sensibilities, a common vocabulary, and a common and collective spiritual bond. It embraced people like my grandmother. It allowed them to read and talk to one another around the neighborhood and community about the issues and happenings of the time. For many of our elders, it allowed them to learn the magic of reading the printed word. They were very proud of reading and teaching their children and grandchildren this art with the Black newspaper. The Black Press influenced our community more than the broader press at one time. *The Chicago Defender* at one point had a readership of more than 500,000, larger than most "white" newspapers' readership.

One of the greatest self-inflicted wounds we currently endure comes from our abandonment of, destruction of, and withdrawal from cultural institutions such as Black newspapers. The loss of many Black institutions from Black life has had a devastating effect on our community. Integration made many Black institutions disappear: Black hospitals (77), Black banks and credit unions (over 100 combined), Black insurance companies (over 50), independent Black-owned movie theaters (over 70), the Negro baseball league (1920–1951), which was a very lucrative "Negro" business in America. The victories of the Civil Rights Movement both helped and hindered Black people. These victories created opportunities for talented Black individuals and hastened the demise of many long-standing Black institutions. We must never forget that institutions are the backbone of peoplehood.

We must hail and salute modern Black journalists who have taken advantage of meaningful opportunities the Civil Rights Movement afforded them. There are now any number of them working for any number of major white daily newspapers and media outlets. Much of this foreword is drawn from their collective courage to challenge white media, from white newspapers to white television news networks to online media. I owe a special debt of gratitude to the likes of Brent Staples, Nikole Hannah-Jones and others who are transforming these juggernaut media conglomerates to recognize Black lives appropriately.

For our future, Black media via Black institutions must be supported, maintained, and developed if we are to maintain our peoplehood, advocate for our interests, and educate our children. Black media makers, personalities, and individuals representing our needs and interests in the broader dominant mass media institutions are very important too, especially when it comes to transforming these spaces into being more pluralistic, human, and representative. The contributors to this anthology share some thought-provoking experiences and ideas about our relationship with the media. Each contributor adds their unique voice to this complex issue of Black people and the media in hopes of elevating our understanding, adding to our collective vocabulary, and challenging us to move as a community with this new knowledge. The brilliant thinkers, scholars, media creators, and institution-builders in this book have local roots and connections to Minnesota, and their voices are national and international. It's a privilege and honor to hear from these fabulous contributors who are defining the next stage of our liberation struggle. This anthology or authoritative text will guide generations on the complex issue of Black people and the media.

Dr. Mahmoud El-Kati

Professor Emeritus of Macalester College
Author of *The Myth of Race/The Reality of Racism* (1st Sankofa Series publication)
Solidarity - Twin Cities

1. I use quotes for emphasis at times and to highlight that, in those instances, I am not referring to the people as white but rather that is a self-definition. This goes for "white" as well as "master" and "slave."

References

Staples, Brent. 2021. "How the White Press Wrote Off Black America." *New York Times,* July 10, 2021. https://www.nytimes.com/2021/07/10/opinion/sunday/white-newspapers-african-americans.html.

Mills, C. Wright. 1956. *The Power Elite.* New York: Oxford University Press.

Contents

1. Authoring A Future in Which We Win — 1
   Al McFarlane

2. Credibility of the Source: How Journalistic Bias Is Slowing Social Progress — 13
   Georgia Fort

3. Black Media and Censorship: A Brief History of White Supremacist "Cancel Culture" — 25
   Dr. Catherine R. Squires

4. Black Media — 33
   Dallas Watson

5. Sticks, Stones, and Words that Hurt: Considering the Revolution Within — 37
   Dr. Danielle K Brown

6. Listening for Black Voices — 45
   Daniel Pierce Bergin

7. Walking in the Footsteps of Uncle Gordon: Keeping the Promise — 53
   Dr. Robin P. Hickman-Winfield

8. Storytelling: More than a Defense Mechanism — 61
   Jasmine Snow

9. Duluth, Minnesota, at a Crossroads: Solutions for Becoming a Beloved Community of the North — 69
   Henry Banks

10. *Minnesota Spokesman-Recorder*: A Family Legacy — 79
    Tracey Williams-Dillard

11. How Publisher Cecil Newman Made His Mark on the Minnesota Newspaper Industry — 95
    Daniel Pierce Bergin

12. Reclaiming My Historical Imagination   101
   Lissa Jones-Lofgren

13. Hear the Children   107
   Donnie Nicole Belcher

14. A Case Study: Frederick Douglass—Literacy and Creating a Voice for His People   113
   Al McFarlane

Appendix   117
   Sankofa Series List of Black Media Books
   MN Black/African American/African Heritage Media Directory

1

Authoring a Future in Which We Win

Al McFarlane

I started my career as a professional journalist in southern Minnesota. I was a student at Worthington Community College and had just returned to the town of 10,000 following the end of a two-year active-duty stint in the US Navy. I was 20 years old. At the community college, I wrote for the school newspaper and became one of the student founders of the *Collage Literary Magazine*. There were two media opportunities available to me at the time: one in radio at the town's commercial station and the path I chose, writing for the *Worthington Daily Globe* part time. As an intern reporter for the *Daily Globe*, I wrote obituaries. My internal sense of humor elevated my noviceship to a stature of life-and-death importance: I said to myself, nobody in Nobles County died without my reporting providing formal public witness to their transition.

The *Daily Globe* won awards nationally for its innovation in printing and use of color photography. It paid close attention to its community as the center of the universe. Local government and education, business and sports, social and religion reporting cradled the AP newswire-enabled global content, and together crafted a view of the world and this community's essential place in it.

I marveled then, and still today, that a town of 10,000 residents could support and be supported by a daily newspaper. The newspaper, to my knowledge, was an extremely profitable enterprise and provided the cohesion that bound the aspirations and comings and goings of events, issues, and ideas out of which the people's identity and opportunity sprang.

So, it has remained perplexing that Minneapolis and St. Paul, with a population in excess of 250,000 Black people, has not created a daily Black newspaper to reflect and serve its identity, opportunity, and aspirations.

After completing my sophomore year of college, I moved to the Twin Cities with the good fortune of having an internship at the *Pioneer Press*, St. Paul's daily morning newspaper. And thanks to my bosses/mentors at the *Daily Globe*, Jim Vance and his brother Bob Vance, I got into the University of Minnesota School of Journalism (J-School) and Mass Communication as the Carl Rowan Journalism Scholar, a scholarship supported by the Ridder family, which owned the *Pioneer Press* and *St. Paul Dispatch* newspapers, among others.

While at the *Pioneer Press*, I wrote about high school sports and then became a general assignment news reporter, which was where I really belonged. At J-School, I became an editor and feature writer for the student publication, *Random Magazine*. And I did a major national piece for *Black Scholar Magazine*, a Q&A interview with master jazz pianist and composer McCoy Tyner.

When I launched *Insight* as a monthly magazine in 1974, I worked for a magazine and commercial printing company, Graphic Services, Inc., in Northeast Minneapolis. I bought the publication from my employer and set out to discover how to create for our community what the *Daily Globe* was for Worthington.

I stand on the shoulders of dragon-slayers, men and women who cast off slavery's shackles in the 1820s and launched a new American tradition for Black people, many of whom were forbidden, by law and custom, the right to read.

A Short History of the Black Press

The bicentennial of the Black Press in the United States is a scant three years from now. The Black Press began in 1827 when John Russwurm and Samuel Cornish started *Freedom's Journal* in New York. By the time the Civil War started, forty Black newspapers were being published. And, during the

1920s and '30s, when white papers virtually ignored Black America, the glory days of the Black Press began.

According to a 2003 article by Larry Muhammad entitled "The Black Press: Past and Present":

> Politics, sports, money and social issues were reported from the perspective of Black readers. The careers of Lena Horne, Little Richard, Paul Robeson, and many other entertainment greats were promoted in their early stages before major media took notice, and editorial writers crusaded for open housing, quality schools, voting rights, fair employment, and equal accommodations—demands that later formed the civil rights agenda. There were bylined stories from America's leading Black activists and intellects—Richard Wright, Gwendolyn Brooks, and Langston Hughes in The *Chicago Defender* and W.E.B. DuBois, Zora Neale Hurston, Marcus Garvey, and Elijah Muhammad in the *Pittsburgh Courier*.
>
> Black publishers grew rich and powerful. Robert S. Abbott started the *Defender* with $13.75 and became one of America's first Black millionaires. By 1929, the *Defender* circulation was 230,000 a week, but the *Pittsburgh Courier* was biggest, topping 300,000 with 15 editions across the country. In 1932, *Courier* publisher Robert L. Vann, Abbott and others steered Black voters in masse to the Democratic Party, breaking traditional ties to the Republican Party of Abraham Lincoln and helping to elect Franklin D. Roosevelt President. Gunnar Myrdal's landmark 1944 study, "An American Dilemma: The Negro Problem and Modern Democracy," said the strongest, most influential institution among Blacks was its crusading press. It set the stage for—and helped engineer—monumental change from school desegregation in 1954 to the voting rights bill of 1957, the marches, sit-ins and civil rights legislation of 1964.

So, the impulse, the urge to be of consequence, to be present in the daily lives of our people was certainly not new. My desires were consistent with the dreams and accomplishments of storied predecessors, colossal giants in

Black newspapering like John Sengstacke, Robert S. Abbot, and Robert L. Vann.

In 2017, journalist Clarene Mitchell wrote:

> In 1827, America viewed and treated Blacks as second-class citizens. Advance the calendar to 2017. The status of African Americans has improved in some regards, but stark disparities remain and continue to worsen. The 2016 presidential election included a candidate whose campaign slogan was "Make America Great Again," but truth be told, America has never been great for Blacks.
>
> Justice for Blacks was boldly championed on March 16, 1827, with the birth of the first Black newspaper, *Freedom's Journal*, which was published as a weekly tabloid in New York City. Although slavery in New York state was abolished that same year, mainstream newspapers brazenly disseminated information that negatively portrayed Blacks. The Rev. Peter Williams, Jr., John B. Russwurm, and Samuel Cornish, frustrated with the distorted representations of their cause, pooled their resources during a meeting in Manhattan to start *Freedom's Journal*. Russwurm was 28 years old and among the first Blacks to graduate from an American university, and Cornish was a preacher.
>
> During the slavery era, slave auction advertisements were commonly seen in newspapers. Images of Blacks during the Jim Crow era were just as brash, exaggerating features and advancing stereotypes. Aunt Jemima represented the overweight, subservient Black woman who was only good for cooking. The Mandingo image perpetuated the notion that Black men were sex crazed and violent. Other images portrayed Black babies as bait for alligators, effectively comparing them to animals. Images of Black people happily eating watermelon and dancing were also widely published. For those Blacks who did not act according to White expectations, images of them enduring beatings in the public square were made into postcards and other novelty items. Blacks could not open a newspaper and read any positive information about themselves or see any images that accurately portrayed them. Issues of importance to their community

were not covered. The founders of *Freedom's Journal* saw the unfair depiction as a grave injustice and an impediment to the advancement of the population. They expressed their commitment to righting this wrong on the pages of the first edition [sic]:

> *We wish to plead our own cause. Too long have others spoken for us. Too long has the public been deceived by misrepresentations, in things which concern us dearly, though in the estimation of some mere trifles; for though there are many in society who exercise towards us benevolent feelings; still (with sorrow we confess it) there are others who make it their business to enlarge upon the least trifle, which tends to the discredit of any person of color; and pronounce anathemas and denounce our whole body for the misconduct of this guilty one. We are aware that there are many instances of vice among us, but we avow that it is because no one has taught its subjects to be virtuous; many instances of poverty, because no sufficient accommodated to minds contracted by slavery, and deprived of early education have been made, to teach them how to husband their hard earnings, and to secure to themselves comfort.*

The Black press began with the sole intention of being a contrast to what was in the White press. The single focus was to represent the Black community in a dignified manner and to shine a positive light on its members' lives. *Freedom's Journal* and the hundreds of Black newspapers that followed it in the 20th century affirmed Black people's existence. Births were announced, deaths were mourned, marriages were celebrated, and achievements were showcased.

In the early days of the Black press, journalists who were shunned by mainstream media gained celebrity status. They have been referred to as "soldiers without swords" because they used their pens, typewriters, and cameras to give voice to the voiceless. The pay was low and the work was hard, but it was more than just a job.

The Black Press Today

Stacy Brown, National Newspaper Publishers Association Newswire senior national correspondent, builds on Mitchell's observations in his 2021 article entitled "Black Press continues to fill void in American journalism." Brown wrote:

> The racial awakening after the death of George Floyd didn't spark a great reaction from mainstream media outlets.
>
> By contrast, Floyd's murder and the global protests that ensued further espoused the importance of the Black Press, and again revealed the dire straits of people of color face if there is no Black Press of America.
>
> Black media continue[s] to create a space where Black folks can speak for ourselves about issues of importance and combat stereotypes that harm us.

In October 2021, a report was released by the Black Media Initiative at the City University of New York's (CUNY) Craig Newmark Graduate School of Journalism. *Called Why Black Media Matters Now*, the report studied 179,865 articles from 97 media sources over a fifteen-month period between March 1, 2020, and May 1, 2021. Black Media Initiative director Cheryl Thompson-Morton highlighted a few findings of the report:

> Black media publishes as much as six times more coverage than mainstream outlets on issues of importance to Black communities, including racism, health disparities, and voting access. Furthermore, it found that nearly one in four articles in Black media mentioned racism or related issues, as compared with less than one in 10 in mainstream media.
>
> Black media "stood out in its focus on a variety of other health issues of particular relevance to Black communities, including maternal health, hypertension, diabetes, HIV/AIDS, and sickle cell disease."

Nearly 200 years later, Black media continue to create a space where Black folks can speak for ourselves about issues of importance and combat stereotypes that harm us.

Black media were important in 1827, and they are just as critical today.

Black media leads the way on stories related to racism, putting focus on these stories at higher levels and earlier in the news cycle than mainstream media.

Black media centers the community in coverage and humanizes the individuals and groups in the news.

Black media connects news events across subjects to cover wider issues of injustice, including threats to voting access, disparities in medical care, and policing and mass incarceration.

Black media provides historical context to present day challenges. This is done by explicitly including historical events in related breaking news, as well as by linking related news events such as police killings of Black people.

The Black Press in the Future

In a world and a nation that is undergoing historic change, a steady and confident force now and in the future is the Black Press. I am encouraged by a recent article describing a collection of Black newspapers uniting to create a new platform: Author Evelyn Mateos, in September 2021, wrote, "Ten Black newspapers have joined forces to create Word In Black, a platform to 'amplify the Black experience by reporting, collecting and sharing stories about real people in communities across our country.'"

Word In Black consists of a newsletter and website (wordinblack.com) that publishes content from ten participating newspapers, which include *New York Amsterdam News*, *The Atlanta Voice*, *Houston Defender Network*, *The Washington Informer*, *Dallas Weekly*, *The Afro*, *Michigan Chronicle*, *The*

Seattle Medium, *The Sacramento Observer*, and *The St. Louis American*. It also publishes original content.

The initiative is part of the Fund for Black Journalism, founded last year by Local Media Association and the same ten newspapers to support coverage and create solutions around issues that affect Black communities.

Nick Charles, project manager for the Fund for Black Journalism and managing director for Word In Black, said the initiative's primary goal is to help these newspapers "survive and thrive."

> "There are over 230 Black-owned newspapers still in this country—here we have 10 of them that still put out a hard copy every week—and what most of them need is a real smooth and efficient transition to digital products," Charles said. The online newsletter has already received 1,200 subscribers. The objective is to build a subscriber base of 500,000 in the next two years. Charles also stated, "Collaboration is going on because people realize that to survive and to meet our mission as journalists, we have to band together."

What is the future of the Black Press? For me, the mission remains as clear and important as when the picture first unfolded in my mind's eye. The collaboration just mentioned above brings into focus pioneering work that I have led and been a part of. Vietnamese brother Nghi Huynh and I in the mid-1980s called on owners of Black, Asian, Latino, and American Indian media to form the Minnesota Minority Media Coalition, which we later renamed as Minnesota Multicultural Media Consortium. Building on the success of that collaboration, I connected with Black newspaper owners in Chicago, Toledo, Milwaukee, and Detroit to create the Midwest Black Publishers Coalition in the early 1990s, a business focused on driving advertising revenue from companies that had a regional footprint.

Today the Twin Cities remain the urban center for Black American space west of Chicago/Milwaukee and east of the Rocky Mountains. Technology now affords us the opportunity to share stories, successes, and challenges not only in our weekly vehicles but instantly, virtually. I believe we are the front line of reimagining a world centered on our Blackness, elevating the beacon that calls all of us home. Home is local and global. It is organic and both timely and timeless. Home celebrates the preciousness of each moment in each of our lives and invites us to value the same . . . it invites us to know ourselves, unfettered and unfiltered, pure, essential.

I believe this book project—a look at the power of the Black Press, really, and a look at the power of the Word—signals our continued emergence into self-discovery and self-confidence and self-awareness, all holding and creating knowledge we can use in service of our prime directive: the pursuit of freedom and relationship-driven actualization.

It is time for a conversation that is fearless, principled, that recognizes and nurtures the dream within, a dream fashioned by culture-informed work, fueled by joy and excitement, trained on solving problems, creating opportunity.

It is time to once again break the shackles that rob our minds and spirits, and see the anticultural sleight of hand for what it is, a deception that stifles self-awareness and attainment, and siphons our existence to fuel ill-gotten advantage at our expense.

So I think about our hands and minds plugged into the digi sphere. We once again are demonstrating our capacity to create the new and the different, beyond myopic expediencies technology tools, apps are created to introduce.

I believe we now must elevate intention, clearing the way for the indwelling spirit of truth to alight and ascend through every element and every moment of our lives. And yes, it is about telling the story. Telling our story. Imagining, and telling a story in which we win. The story is the map that gets us from there to here, the place of infinity.

References

Brown, Stacy. 2021. "Black Press continues to fill void in American journalism." *St. Louis American*, October 14, 2021. https://www.stlamerican.com/news/editorials/black-press-continues-to-fill-void-in-american-journalism/.

Mateos, Evelyn. Ten Black Newspapers Unite to Create Platform that Amplifies the Black Experience, (Interview with Nick Charles). *The Tennessee Tribune*, September 5, 2021. https://tntribune.com/ten-black-newspapers-unite-to-create-platform-that-amplifies-the-black-experience/

Mitchell, Clarene. 2017. "Why We Need an All-Black Press," A Women's Thing (blog). September 20, 2017. https://awomensthing.org/blog/why-we-need-the-black-press/.

Muhammad, Larry. 2003. "The Black Press: Past and Present," *Journalism and Black America: Then and Now*. Cambridge, MA: Nieman Reports. September 15, 2003. https://niemanreports.org/articles/the-black-press-past-and-present/.

Thompson-Morton, Cheryl. 2021. "Why Black Media Matters Now." New York, NY: Craig Newmark Graduate School of Journalism's Center for Community Media. October 6, 2021. https://blackmediareport.journalism.cuny.edu/.

Al McFarlane

Elder Al McFarlane is editor in chief of *Insight News* and CEO at McFarlane Media Interests Inc. both housed at the Marcus Garvey House in North Minneapolis. He is a journalist, news reporter, editor, content creator, and curator of many multimedia vehicles such as the partnership with KFAI radio hosting weekly *Conversations with Al McFarlane*, which also is a daily podcast. *Insight News* is also on the World Wide Web and serves not only Minnesota but the African diaspora with its outreach and news content. Elder McFarlane works in the proud Black Press tradition of courageous journalism, creating a historical record and a Black perspective, which serves as a knowledge foundation for future generations and serves as a catalyst for changing our society. Al McFarlane is the editor for this anthology publication about the Black community and the media.

2

Credibility of the Source: How Journalistic Bias Is Slowing Social Progress

Georgia Fort

In examining the media's relationship with Black America, you'll find a painful yet teachable history, in which newspapers wrought destruction on majority-Black communities and in which editors precipitated the torture and lynching of countless Black men and women. We know journalism's mission well: to provide balanced, fair, and unbiased reporting to inform the public. However, over several decades, the nation's news organizations did the opposite at the expense of Black lives. Though the methods have become more nuanced, that same partiality exists today. Untruths are still finding their way to front pages and the murders of innocent Black folks are being justified to this day. All of this—the unverified details, the prejudiced framing, the reliance on police departments for key information—directly contradicts journalistic values and puts millions of marginalized people at risk.

At the core of the problem is an erosion of the media industry's moralistic foundation. An impurity at the root of the business is poisoning the practice, its ethical limbs falling off one by one. We lack mass media reform and narrative justice. With the gutting of smaller presses, the consolidation of major publishing houses, and the proliferation of misinformation on social media, we've lost sight of how to enforce a journalistic code of ethics. There's no industry standard that ensures we're getting the truth; it's much easier to find news sources that reinforce your belief system, and it's also easier to turn in shoddy reporting without consequence.

But even if the journalists, their editors, and their employers don't feel the sting, our community does, resulting not just in bad journalism but sponsored terrorism at the hands of the institutions we're meant to trust most.

The Pillars of Journalism

Readers maintain high expectations of mainstream media because the industry abides by an official code of ethics as outlined by the Society of Professional Journalists (2014). On day one, we may not be sworn in officially, but in taking up the gauntlet of the press, we're committing to these standards. Among them, we must seek truth and report it, minimize harm, act independently, and be both accountable and transparent. Contained within these pillars are many nuances, including the need to provide appropriate context, consider sources' motives, and identify those sources clearly.

Journalism can only be a trusted institution because of these values and ethics, and a tremendous part of maintaining our objectivity comes from citing credible sources. What does "credible" mean? A credible source is trustworthy, and their story can be verified by other means. A credible source doesn't have an ax to grind, or if they do, we're aware of it and account for the bias by finding sources on the other side. A credible source is just as interested in unveiling the truth as we are.

Our industry depends on these credible sources because there's often no other way to get to the heart of the stories we tell. But when sources prove to be unreliable or deceitful—regardless of who they are or how authoritative they may be—they jeopardize the quality of our work. Sadly, throughout history credible sources have been scarce when it comes to white journalists reporting about the Black community, making coverage about us questionable at best and deadly at worst.

Tulsa to Now—Misinformation and Racial Violence

Officially, the events of the 1921 Tulsa Race Massacre were set in motion when Dick Rowland, a Black teenager, stepped into the Drexel Building elevator with a white woman named Sarah Page. Exactly what transpired between them remains unknown, but rumors quickly spread that Rowland had committed a crime against Page. White rioters soon took to the Greenwood District, razing Black Wall Street, killing as many as three hundred people, and destroying hundreds of millions of dollars in generational wealth (Tulsa Historical Society and Museum 2022).

In this retelling, one detail is often overlooked: a sensational report in the May 31, 1921, edition of *The Tulsa Tribune*. The headline, "Nab N**** for Attacking Girl in Elevator," was not unbiased, balanced, or verified for accuracy. It was a call to arms that incited a white mob to kill hundreds of people, inflict racial terror, and decimate millions in Black wealth—all because of an unsubstantiated allegation.

Despite no official account of the supposed incident, the paper reported that Rowland was arrested for sexually assaulting Page (History.com 2021). That fuel was what lit the fire. Before burning down Greenwood, the angry white mob descended on the local courthouse where Rowland was being jailed. Several Black residents showed up on two separate occasions to protect him but, outnumbered and overpowered, they fled home and the white mob followed.

What did or didn't occur between Rowland and Page was already a source of controversy without official commentary. But the newspaper's incendiary, unscrupulous work inflamed tensions, causing an eruption that changed the course of American history.

We'd never imagine such a blatant display of racism in newspapers today. There are journalistic norms and expectations of fairness and accuracy. Reporting a crime without official verification, stoking racial divisions just to move copies, publishing falsehoods without any accountability for the violence or unrest that results—these certainly seem like behaviors of the past. Yet this bias remains rooted in our journalistic standards and directly contributes to a lack of social progress and narrative justice today.

In many American newsrooms, it's assumed that police departments, their chiefs, their officers, and the city officials who support them can be trusted, at all costs, without scrutiny. But in Minneapolis, a community where I work as an independent journalist, the Minneapolis Police Department (MPD) has been anything but dependable.

Amir Locke was killed by police during a no-knock warrant in February 2022, and almost immediately, the MPD tried to shift public opinion in its favor. Shortly after the shooting, the department released photos of Locke's handgun without the context that he was a licensed gun owner well within his legal rights to possess a firearm (WCCO CBS Minnesota 2022). Interim Chief Amelia Huffman initially said Locke had pointed his gun at officers after they entered, but bodycam footage contradicted her claims (Uren 2022). In MPD's first press release after the killing, Locke was referred to as a suspect despite not being named in the warrant.

MPD attempted to shape the public narrative about Locke through misinformation and outright lies. It was an obvious attempt to lower the heat on a department that has remained under the national microscope since the killing of George Floyd. In protecting their necks, they also dehumanized and criminalized a victim who did nothing wrong. Locke wasn't a criminal; he was a young man who simply happened to be in the right place at the wrong time.

Unfortunately, there's a through line from the Tulsa Race Massacre to Locke, and that is source credibility. In 1921, no source could verify what happened between Rowland and Page, yet, thanks to *The Tulsa Tribune*, Rowland was found guilty in the court of public opinion. In the case of Locke, MPD fed the press information that would seemingly justify his killing. Without modern-day body cam footage and protests, the department may have succeeded.

In the decades between the inflammatory reporting in the *Tribune* and the MPD's misinformation about Locke, there are countless examples of white newspaper owners weaponizing the press to inflict harm on Black men, women, and communities. Several of these stories have been gathered in the *Printing Hate* digital exhibit from the University of Maryland's Howard

Center for Investigative Journalism. For instance, George White was lynched in Delaware on June 23, 1903, just seven days after he was accused of fatally assaulting the daughter of a local minister (Adefiwitan 2022). Three different Delaware newspapers printed information about the case, painting White as guilty right away. One of those papers, *The News Journal*, told readers where White was being held. Another, *The Evening Journal*, published excerpts from the minister's sermon about whether or not White should be lynched. He was dragged from jail and burned alive less than 48 hours after that issue hit the streets.

Zooming out, there was a litany of white-owned papers across the country that regularly incited violence, eschewing the responsibility to inform for a brand of sensationalism that cost many Black citizens their lives (Brown 2021).

We can see the historical roots of printed hate in the MPD's actions and those of other police departments throughout America. In the first press release after Floyd's death, police said he died following a "medical incident" during a police interaction (Levenson 2021). We now know the medical incident was former officer Derek Chauvin's knee on his neck. And just this year, a Minnesota Department of Human Rights (2022) investigation found that MPD engaged in a longtime pattern of race discrimination, confirming what Black residents have known and experienced for decades.

Similarly, during the summer of racial justice protests in 2020, police officers in Buffalo, New York, claimed a peaceful protester fell and struck his head, but video revealed he was shoved by police. In Philadelphia, police beat a Temple University student with a metal baton after claiming he'd assaulted an officer; video proved this false, and prosecutors went after the officer instead (Associated Press 2020). In 2019, the Louisiana State Patrol said Ronald Greene died in a car crash; this narrative was published as fact until, years later, body camera footage showed that police brutally beat him to death and covered it up by lying about it (Mustian and Bleiberg 2022). Or what about Winston Smith, a Black man fatally shot by law enforcement? The first article published by the *Star Tribune* wrongfully identified him as a murder suspect (*Minneapolis Star Tribune* 2021).

So, given this history—of newspapers fomenting violence against Black communities and police departments dehumanizing and criminalizing Black victims—why aren't news outlets more suspicious of police sources?

Credibility of the Source

Inexplicably, many mainstream media outlets turn a blind eye to the fact that police department sources are increasingly unreliable. This blindness is in direct opposition to journalistic values. We must verify facts across multiple sources; we are never to take a single source as an absolute authority on any issue, especially if that source has direct involvement in the incident in question.

Despite our duty to think critically about weighty subjects before reporting them, many news organizations aren't considering police departments' motives. We live in a heated and polarized political climate, in which there are calls to defund departments and there's less trust in police. Officers have an incentive to curate a positive public image, but this typically comes at the expense of the marginalized.

What we're seeing in newsrooms is a valorization of police and an assumption that they can be trusted full stop because they represent the law. However, bias and malpractice can exist in any field, policing not excluded. This truth has been exhibited again and again, most acutely since 2020 with the death of Floyd and other high-profile police killings. By reporting on police brutality this way, with the perpetrators of violence and misinformation acting as key sources, the media only reinforces the power imbalance between law enforcement and Black communities. They also embed their work with racism and bias, and they enable the continued modern-day lynching of Black men. Lynching may not be what it was at the time of the Tulsa Race Massacre, but even by different means, the killing of unarmed and innocent Black men under false pretenses is lynching. And allowing police departments to justify those lynchings on the front pages of newspapers sends a message that it's permissible.

Furthermore, there's no focus on narrative justice or any kind of reconciliation for the well-documented harm caused by inaccurate narratives at our most prominent outlets. The smaller and less standardized the publication, the less incentive to tell stories that humanize people of color and present fair, balanced accounts of hot-button issues. There's rarely an acknowledgment of the role racism and discrimination play not just in the stories reported, but in who gets hired to tell them. That's likely due to the lack of representation in many of the country's most influential newsrooms.

Thus, it's no surprise that trust in the media is declining to record lows. The number of Americans who have a "great deal" or "fair amount" of trust and confidence in news reporting barely surpasses the 2016 figure, which was the lowest on record (Brenan 2021). Nor is it surprising that news organizations, especially smaller titles, are struggling to survive. More than one hundred local newsrooms shuttered during the pandemic (Hare 2021).

But these journalistic deficiencies aren't just chipping away at news subscriptions. They're also directly linked to stalled progress in the social justice movement. The year 2020 seemed like a flashpoint as protests swept the country and the globe; yet the summer of reckoning led to incremental policing changes at best (Subramanian and Arzy 2021). Even right here in Minneapolis, where the movement touched off, voters declined to enact major police reform when given the chance (Oladipo 2021). One can only imagine stronger support behind police accountability if Black victims were consistently reported on in humanizing ways and if sources other than police were controlling the narrative—or at minimum the media was presenting balanced reporting that included families' voices alongside law enforcement agencies.

A More Balanced Way Forward

Moving toward a fairer, more balanced journalistic future will take tremendous work, but it's possible, and it starts with meaningful action from both the media and the audience.

Journalists, editors, and news organizations need a unified definition of media reform, one which includes consistent enforcement of journalistic ethics and punishment for those who violate the established standards. A major pillar of these reform efforts must address sourcing, including fully researching source backgrounds and only deeming information fact once it has been verified by multiple entities. They should also address newsroom diversity to ensure a variety of reporting perspectives and to uplift underrepresented voices and lived experiences.

Readers have a duty to hold news outlets accountable, too. Mechanisms like letters to the editor and formal complaints to watchdog organizations can call attention to ethical lapses and reporting biases. They must declare harmful, inaccurate narratives invalid and advocate for truth in all forms of media, which also requires pushback against the right wing–led movement to remove race– and social justice–centered education from US schools.

Going even further, we must completely reimagine journalism to undo the terror and peril of decades past and ensure a media future that informs, values, and protects communities of color.

What does journalism look like if we no longer use police departments as sources? So often we default to law enforcement for everything from shootings and car accidents to fires. But why? Exactly how many lies must a source tell until they're no longer considered credible? At what point can a journalist label an agency "corrupt" for maliciously covering up its wrongdoings and engaging in discriminatory practices that take Black lives? Journalism without dependence on police sources looks like speaking to victims and witnesses and painting fuller, more humanized narratives. Journalism without dependence on police sources looks like decreased focus on petty crime and greater elevation of positive stories. Journalism without dependence on police sources looks a lot like the version of ethical reporting we're all expected to uphold.

What does journalism look like if newsrooms value their journalists of color instead of forcing them to conform to Eurocentric language standards? These writers could tell their stories with authenticity and open up previously exclusionary publications and programming to the audiences most impacted by their reporting. Diversity would be more than a statistic or a box to check on an organizational to-do list. These storytellers would be appreciated for their unique points of view and allowed to explore connections to communities and events. They could report as their whole selves and serve their readership, not just the names on the masthead.

And what does journalism look like if there's narrative justice? For all the Black men and women whose names were falsely linked to crimes like murder, rape, and theft, who eventually gained freedom but endured years and years of reputational damage, what reparations are sufficient? What does journalism look like if media outlets acknowledge the violence, slander, narrative criminalization, and dehumanization they've inflicted on our communities? How will those stories be told, who will tell them, and when will we know that the media has done enough? Is there such a thing as enough?

We can all take actions to create the journalistic future we expect, but what we really need is a transformative shift. We must step forward fearlessly into a mode of reporting that no longer requires police cooperation; we must treat newsroom diversity as a pathway to richer, more representative reporting; and we must fight for a quantifiable narrative justice that atones for historical inequities while safeguarding the future for subjects of color. The status quo isn't only passé, it's unsustainable, and there's no time for slow and steady evolution. We must demand rapid, unequivocal change *now*—our lives depend on it.

References

Adefiwitan, Anuoluwapo. 2022. "A lynching countenanced by the white press and church." *Printing Hate*, Howard Center for Investigative Journalism, University of Maryland. January 24, 2022. https://lynching.cnsmaryland.org/2022/01/23/a-lynching-countenanced-by-the-white-press-and-church/.

Associated Press. 2020. "Video evidence increasingly disproves police narratives." MPR News, June 9, 2020. https://www.mprnews.org/story/2020/06/09/video-evidence-increasingly-disproves-police-narratives.

Brenan, Megan. 2021. "Americans' Trust in Media Dips to Second Lowest on Record." Gallup, October 7, 2021. https://news.gallup.com/poll/355526/americans-trust-media-dips-second-lowest-record.aspx.

Brown, DeNeen. 2021. "For scores of years, newspapers printed hate, leading to racist terror lynchings and massacres of Black Americans." *Printing Hate*, Howard Center for Investigative Journalism, University of Maryland. October 18, 2021. https://lynching.cnsmaryland.org/2021/10/12/printing-hate-newspapers-lynching/.

Hare, Kristen. 2021. "More than 100 local newsrooms closed during the coronavirus pandemic." Poynter, December 2, 2021. https://www.poynter.org/locally/2021/the-coronavirus-has-closed-more-than-100-local-newsrooms-across-america-and-counting/.

History.com. 2021. "Tulsa Race Massacre." May 26, 2021.

Levenson, Eric. 2021. "How Minneapolis Police first described the murder of George Floyd, and what we know now." CNN, April 21, 2021. https://www.cnn.com/2021/04/21/us/minneapolis-police-george-floyd-death/index.html.

Minneapolis Star Tribune. 2021. "Correction on Uptown shooting." June 9, 2021. https://www.startribune.com/correction-on-uptown-shooting/600066525/.

Minnesota Department of Human Rights. 2022. Investigation Findings. April 27, 2022. https://mn.gov/mdhr/mpd/findings/.

Mustian, Jim, and Jake Bleiberg. 2022. "'Torture and murder': Ronald Greene case turns cop vs. cop." AP, March 22, 2002. https://apnews.com/article/death-of-ronald-greene-louisiana-arrests-scott-brown-ronald-greene-a87d22256aecadcee00540b9f492b78d.

Oladipo, Gloria. 2021. "Minneapolis voters reject bid to replace police with public safety department." *The Guardian*, November 2, 2021. https://www.theguardian.com/us-news/2021/nov/02/minneapolis-police-department-vote-result.

Society of Professional Journalists. 2014. *SPJ Code of Ethics*. September 6, 2014. https://www.spj.org/ethicscode.asp.

Subramanian, Ram, and Leily Arzy. 2021. "State Policing Reforms Since George Floyd's Murder." Brennan Center For Justice, May 21, 2021. https://www.brennancenter.org/our-work/research-reports/state-policing-reforms-george-floyds-murder.

Tulsa Historical Society and Museum. 2022. 1921 Tulsa Race Massacre.https://www.tulsahistory.org/exhibit/1921-tulsa-race-massacre/#flexible-content.

Tulsa Tribune. 1921. "Nab N**** for Attacking Girl in Elevator." May 31, 1921.

Uren, Adam. 2022. "Minneapolis police union issues new statement on Amir Locke killing." Bring Me The News, February 5, 2022. https://bringmethenews.com/minnesota-news/minneapolis-police-union-issues-new-statement-on-amir-locke-killing.

WCCO CBS Minnesota. 2022. "Amir Locke Fatal Shooting by MPD: What We Know (And Don't Know) So Far." February 8, 2020. https://minnesota.cbslocal.com/2022/02/08/man-killed-in-mpd-shooting-what-we-know-and-dont-know-so-far/#whatpolicesay.

Georgia Fort

Georgia Fort is a two-time Midwest Emmy Award-winning journalist. She was one of two journalists in the courtroom for the sentencing of Derek Chauvin. Her reporting has been published on CNN, ABC, NBC, Fox, and CBS affiliates. Her mission as a storyteller is to change the narrative by amplifying truth, citing diverse sources, and contextualizing social justice issues. Since 2019 Georgia has actively produced and published digital content independently in efforts to activate her own platform, create opportunities for other creators, and be a pioneer of the future of news. Her work ethic and powerful approach to storytelling allowed her to launch her own independent TV news program, *"Here's the Truth,"* which has aired three seasons on the CW Twin Cities. In 2020, she worked as a field producer for NBC's *Today Show* online where she helped create a piece about the Say Their Names Cemetery in Minneapolis and contributed to PBS Frontline's *American Voices*.

Georgia is a mother of three girls and wife of former pro-boxer and gym owner Cerresso Fort.

3

Black Media and Censorship: A Brief History of White Supremacist "Cancel Culture"

Dr. Catherine R. Squires

The history of Black Americans and media is clear on at least two issues: First, Black people have consistently operated as innovators and boundary breakers, both within the confines of white-dominated media firms and as independent creators, critics, and entrepreneurs. Second, in every type of media, Black people have faced censorship forces that threatened both their ability to broadcast their opinions, experiences, and truthful accounts of racism in the United States and their very lives. This essay recounts three historical moments when Black American media producers were targeted by the government, white supremacist organizations, or mobs that sought to silence their voices or end their lives for expressing themselves and speaking truth to power. This selection of incidents is by no means exhaustive but hopefully illustrates how persistent and dangerous white resistance has been to the dissemination of Black media throughout American history, across media genres and technologies. Indeed, amidst today's controversies about so-called "cancel culture," we would do well to remember how vehemently white organizations and government officials have canceled Black media.

The Great Escape: Ida B. Wells

Ida B. Wells may not have lived to be the legend she became had a white mob had its way in 1892. The fearless teacher, newspaper editor, and columnist had built a reputation as a truth-teller in Memphis, Tennessee, writing for the *Free Speech & Headlight.* She relentlessly exposed corruption wherever she saw it, from the segregated school system to voter suppression. Wells, of course, is most famous for her unrelenting coverage of lynching. When a white mob lynched the Black owners of the People's Grocery, she wrote a scathing column that directly addressed the lies and greed that had driven mob violence against Black entrepreneurs who sought economic independence from white businesses. Then she departed on a train for New York to meet with T. Thomas Fortune, editor and publisher of *The New York Age*. Thomas knew her work would electrify his readers and wanted her to write for him.

The timing of her trip was perfect.

Soon after she departed, a mob of white citizens attacked the offices of the *Free Speech*, where they broke all the equipment and ransacked the building. Had she been in Memphis that night, she likely would have become another lynching victim. Fortunately for her and for the Black public, she survived and thrived as a journalist, Civil Rights leader, and orator. But like so many Black journalists, her life was often in danger and attempts to silence her continued in overt and subtle ways. Wells did not return to Memphis for thirty years given the dangers there. And when she wasn't physically threatened, she was attacked by white journalists who called her a "slandering mulattress." In the same vein, white-led women's rights organizations refused to permit her and other Black women leaders to join in or speak at their suffrage events. Wells' career is a testament to the necessity of fostering and sustaining independent Black media outlets; had they not existed, much of her work never would have seen the light of day or been read by more than a handful of folks.

Sidetracking Censorship: *The Chicago Defender* and the Pullman Porters

Historians such as Lee Finkle, Patrick Washburn, and documentary filmmaker Stanley Nelson have illustrated how much pressure government entities put on the Black Press, pushing them to cease or minimize their criticism of Jim Crow in the first four decades of the twentieth century. Between 1917 and 1945, federal agencies, most prominently the FBI and the Office of War Information, habitually targeted Black newspapers such as *The Chicago Defender* for alleged acts of sedition. The charge was that editorials against lynching, poll taxes, and other aspects of Jim Crow oppression were "unpatriotic" and would undermine government authority and public confidence in a time of war. For a time, many Army bases would not allow Black soldiers to maintain subscriptions to Black newspapers. Some officials believed Black soldiers would desert the armed forces if they read too much about lynchings or underfunded segregated schools in the *Defender* or *The Pittsburgh Courier*.

The FBI and other agencies put the Black Press under investigation. And they deputized others to help them. FBI leaders viewed white local officials in the South as "experts" in "their Negroes." Thus, the FBI relied on local sheriffs, postmasters, and others to report on suspicious activity, including reading habits. Several local governments took advantage of the federal government's assault on Black Americans' exercise of the First Amendment not just to suppress antiracist speech but also to preserve their power over sharecroppers and other exploited Black workers who were beginning to leave the South for educational opportunities and better wages in northern cities.

Local white leaders tried to stem the tide of what would later be called the Great Black Migration. They knew Black workers read about jobs in the *Defender* and other northern papers. Some counties and town councils passed laws outlawing the sale of Black newspapers; others turned a blind eye to mob violence against Black newspaper sellers and readers. Under the guise of patriotism, Black people were beaten, even shot for daring to read or distribute the news. Through this mix of brutality and selective interpretation of anti-sedition laws, white officials hoped to cut off the inflow of independent Black information and the outflow of cheap labor, and stifle any hint of dissent against racial apartheid.

But Jim Crow officials and local thugs couldn't prevent the papers from getting through. When he realized what was happening in the South, *Defender* publisher Robert S. Abbott turned to one of the most powerful networks of Black Americans in the country: the Pullman porters. Abbott and his editors were familiar with the porters, some of whom wrote for the

Defender or provided news tips to reporters who couldn't travel South. Abbott asked the porters to smuggle copies of the *Defender* on the trains and drop them off between official stops for local Black folks to pick up in secret.

As Nelson's film *The Black Press: Soldiers Without Swords* illustrates so well, white officials never anticipated the stealth activism of the Pullman porters. Most white people who traveled by train viewed the Pullman porters as happy and subservient, with no purpose in life other than to serve white travelers. But they were wrong: Many porters were college educated but segregation and racism kept them from being able to pursue careers outside the service industry. As such, they were able to hide in plain sight, feeding the Black public news and information that helped keep hope alive and light pathways to escape the South.

Fear of a Black Planet: Black Music vs. Legal & Mob Intimidation

Any survey of American popular music reveals the importance of Black artists and genres born from the cultural traditions of the African diaspora. However, when recorded music and radio were emerging as technologies, American music producers and sellers worked hard to maintain segregation in sound. Music historians such as Brian Ward, Maureen Mahon, and Reebee Garofalo have demonstrated how record companies either refused to record Black artists or had separate labels that visually identified a song as a "race record," meaning a song performed by a Black artist. Many radio stations refused to play "race records." Music halls and theaters segregated their schedules to keep white audiences away from Black musicians.

Obviously, these attempts at segregating music were futile, but they continued for decades, supported not only by the music industry but also by the US government and white supremacist organizations. Ward documented multiple incidents of legal tactics and physical violence deployed against Black musicians. In 1957, then-Senator John F. Kennedy requested an article condemning the immoral influence of rock 'n' roll music be included in the *Congressional Record*. Chuck Berry, whom many consider the Father of Rock 'n' Roll, reported he often had to run for his life from a venue because a mob had gathered to beat him up. According to the segregationists, just playing Black music was equivalent to encouraging interracial sex. Thus, police charged the doo-wop group the Platters with soliciting prostitution when they found white fans mixing with Black fans at one of their shows. When the group was brought before the judge, they were acquitted, but the judge took the time to lambast the Platters for being part of a "socially abhorrent" activity.

In addition to trying to keep live performances segregated, white supremacists also took aim at radio stations that played a mix of Black and white artists. They believed Black music could infect their communities via recordings and radio. A mob in Texas destroyed a jukebox installed at a whites-only pool. Why? Because there were records by Black artists in the jukebox, virtually violating the segregation edict. Similarly, members of the Ku Klux Klan severely damaged the transmitter of WEDR-Birmingham for playing R&B records. Another white supremacist sued WSIX, a station in Nashville, Tennessee, alleging that by playing rock 'n' roll the station had violated federal communication laws against "indecency" on the air. In 1958, the judge agreed and issued an injunction against the station ordering them to replace the rock 'n' roll with more suitable, decent fare.

Beyond the violent reaction to the music itself, there were also barriers preventing Black people from owning and operating radio stations. The Federal Communications Commission (FCC) regularly refused license applications from Black business owners and entrepreneurs. The first Black-owned radio station didn't take to the air until 1949, when Atlanta University professor Jesse Blayton Sr. bought WERD-Atlanta. Though in 1948 WDIA in Memphis had famously hired Black DJs to appeal to the large Black population there, until WERD there were no Black-owned stations in the United States. In the early 1970s, the Congressional Black Caucus pushed for reforms in FCC licensing procedures, finally pushing Black radio ownership into the double digits. Still, today, after decades of deregulation of broadcasting, fewer than one percent of radio stations are Black-owned.

Today, we hear multiple echoes of these not-so-distant historical events. In Florida, Texas, and other states, legislatures have passed laws banning books that take a close look at slavery and Jim Crow. Bans on critical race theory and other alleged "un-American" theories have taken hold of school boards, and conservative pundits are on a witch hunt to root out writers and speakers who explain why our society still hasn't fully reckoned with the rot of racism. Journalist Nikole Hannah-Jones, whose *1619 Project* brought the nation a powerful means of reckoning with the continuing impacts of slavery and white supremacy, has been besieged by death threats—just like Ida B. Wells. As new media technologies evolve and old media mechanisms persist, Black people must continue to fight attempts to block us from creating and sharing our own analyses, opinions, histories, and art. Clearly, the white supremacist drive to censor Black voices and historical truths is not relenting.

References

Bay, Mia. 2010. *To Tell the Truth Freely: The Life of Ida B. Wells*. New York: Hill and Wang.

Nelson, Stanely, director. 1999. *The Black Press: Soldiers Without Swords* (film).

Ward, Brian. 1998. *Just My Soul Responding: Rhythm and Blues, Black Consciousness, and Race Relations*. Berkeley, CA: University of California Press.

Dr. Catherine R. Squires

Dr. Catherine R. Squires retired in 2022 from her position as Associate Dean of the Humphrey School of Public Affairs at the University of Minnesota. Professor Squires is the author of multiple books and articles on media, race, gender, and politics, including *Dispatches from the Color Line* (2007) and *The Post-Racial Mystique* (2014), and editor of the collection *Dangerous Discourses: Feminism, Gun Violence, and Civic Life* (2016). She has engaged in multiple community partnerships in the Twin Cities to uplift and share local Black histories, support BIPOC writers, curate panels, host conferences, and facilitate intergenerational story sharing.

Dr. Squires earned her PhD in Communication Studies from Northwestern University. Prior to finishing her PhD, she was a doctoral fellow in the Center for Black Studies Research at the University of California, Santa Barbara (1998-99). In 1999 she began her first faculty position at the University of Michigan, Ann Arbor, and in 2007 she was hired as the inaugural Cowles Professor of Journalism, Diversity, and Equality at the University of Minnesota School of Journalism and Mass Communication. She lives in St. Paul with her family and is always on the lookout for interesting birds.

4

Black Media

Dallas Watson

What is Black media to me? Black media is for us by us. It is our perspective of Black culture. It is Black Twitter, *The Breakfast Club*, Lil Baby, Drake, Don Lemon, Oprah, and Gayle King. Black media is Druski, Desi Banks, Funky Dineva, and Local Black Child. Black media is all of us. Movies like *Barbershop*, *The Best Man*, *Juice*, *Soul Food*, *Love & Basketball*, and *Coming to America* portrayed the Black experience in multifaceted ways. Black media is what is popular and what is real. Black media has the power to shut down companies and create movements for social justice.

As a young person, my first introduction to Black media was on the school bus in the third grade listening to Rae Sremmurd. I remember feeling out of place because this was my first time actively listening to rap or hip-hop. I had just moved from my home of St. Paul, Minnesota, to East St. Louis, Illinois, and was adjusting to the culture. I was now around a city filled with an abundance of Black kids and adults in my community. There were new hairdos that I had never known about, new sayings that I had never spoken, and new music that was more soulful and heartfelt. I was starting to embrace my Blackness. I was exposed to Black music, Black writers, and Black history. I read for the first time *The Narrative of Sojourner Truth* in the third grade. My teachers would never understand how powerful it was for me to be around other Black students, which allowed me to celebrate and expand my Blackness. Listening to hip-hop, watching Black Girls Rock on BET, and learning about my history allowed me to feel confident in my Black identity. What folks tend to forget, though, is that Black media is community. It is not just one area or theme but rather a diverse group of people. Through music, art, television, news, and podcasts, people share their stories and shed light on their home, and their place of being. These stories are the real-life experiences of Black people all over the world.

Black media is around all of us. We set the trends and are the juice. There is an illusion that Black media is just Oprah, Don Lemon, Gayle King, Al Sharpton, Jesse Jackson, etc. What we wear, what we say, and what we do has the power to shift markets, move industries, and create national movements. Black media can change the culture with a push of a button. It is revolutionary in that way. Movements like Black Lives Matter and Colin Kaepernick's stance on the NFL were created and elevated with the Black media's push to change unequal systems in the world. Black media has the power to speak to people, to mobilize, and to protest injustice in this world.

Black media allowed me to leave my reality. I remember as a young person listening to *The Breakfast Club* and it was my safe space. It was a radio show where I could feel like I mattered. I was tuning in everyday listening to these three Black journalists talk about funny and authentic issues about the Black community. They would have artists, entertainers, newscasters, and actresses shed light on their lives. It would be funny, and sometimes serious, with a splash of brutal honesty. In each episode, I felt like it was my escape from the real world. Being an Awkward Black Girl like Issa Rae, I felt like *The Breakfast Club* was my escape from life. Black media made me laugh and remember where I was from.

Throughout middle school and high school I was bullied for my sexuality. I lived in a rural area, where a lot of my classmates were very similar and folks who were different were not in the majority. Looking back on it, I would listen to *The Breakfast Club* to escape into the hosts' reality. I could listen to a Black brother talk about how he went to Columbia University, or hear about how Charlamagne tha God was beefing with Beanie Sigel, and then listen to Dame Dash speak about how he could never have a boss! Black media meant that I could be celebrated by hearing their experiences and outlook on life. It was my way to leave my space, my room, and venture into the news and stories of Black people around the world.

As I have gotten older, my escape has become music. I moved back to Minnesota for college, where I attend Macalester College. Being there at times I missed my Black roots and my Black peers. I missed my African American Vernacular English always being understood. I missed the bar-b-ques and the down South sayings. Most of all, I missed that folks looked like me. I still have this desire to find my Black community, and so I have turned to music. I love to listen to Maxwell, Brian McKnight, Meek Mill, Kirk Franklin, etc. Black music makes me feel as though I am with my Black community even though I am thousands of miles away from home. Little things like listening to Shannon Sharpe or Deion Sanders make me feel that I am right next to my uncles or my cousins. That is why Black media is so important, because we get to tell our own stories on our own terms. We do not have to change for the world, but we get to show our authentic story and be exactly who we are.

Black media is a community. Though every artist, journalist, creator, and influencer do not know each other, they still represent one another. They look like one another and I believe that is what makes Black media so influential and dope. I can turn on the TV and see Stephen A. Smith roasting a football player because he did not make the right tackle. I can go on YouTube and hear Eric Thomas talk about his life and how it took him twelve years to get a college degree. I can flip on my phone and listen to the *Earn Your Leisure* podcast and hear them talk about generational wealth for the Black community. At the end of the day, Black media is for us by us. It tells our stories from our point of view. It changes the culture with every post, upload, and meme. Black media is revolutionary power. It has the power to give voice to Black culture and Black people. Most of all, Black media shares our stories and lives to celebrate, uplift, and change the world.

Dallas Watson

Dallas Jewell Watson is an undergraduate student in her second year at Macalester College in St. Paul, Minnesota. She is a member of Delta Sigma Theta Sorority, Inc., and Known MPLS. She is the cofounder of Auntie & Z, an intergenerational space for the younger generation to talk and learn from their elders. Her current scholarly interests are Africana studies, geography, urban studies, and American studies. Dallas is the recipient of the QuestBridge National College Match, the Gilman International Scholar Award, and the East St. Louis NAACP Oratory competition awards. She is also a contributor to the book *Reauthoring Savage Inequalities: Narratives of Community Cultural Wealth in Urban Educational Environments*.

5

Sticks, Stones, and Words that Hurt: Considering the Revolution Within

Dr. Danielle K. Brown

Most of us know that sticks, stones, and words can hurt you. But, compared to the bruises left from sticks and stones, communication, storytelling, and narratives yield unique power. Narratives keep records, shape cultures, and influence policy. Narratives can embrace and erase ideas, experiences, and progress. Stories can influence human behavior and encourage people to connect, share, and mobilize. What exists in the dominant narrative can define how society works. For Black communities, the mainstream media's dominant portrayals have long been connected with words and images that hurt. This chapter will discuss this past and center Black communities, in all their varied forms, as a space for moving forward.

The mainstream news media have wielded narratives that have hurt Black communities for decades. Time and time again, news coverage adheres to stereotypes and familiar stories that dehumanize Black people and frame calls for justice as threats to everyday life. In line with the findings from researchers, critics, and ancestors of the past, my research on police violence and protests has found that the media failed by delivering an overall narrative that promoted harm to Black people and prevented justice. Since the antiracism movement was reenergized in the early 2010s, media narratives have focused excessively on sticks and stones, fires, property destruction, emotional outrage, and criminalizing descriptions of victims of police violence and the protests that follow their deaths. Such was the case in analyses of national and local media coverage of the killing of Michael Brown, Eric Garner, and Tamir Rice. And again after the death of

Sandra Bland, Freddie Gray, Alton Sterling, Philando Castile, and Stephon Clark.

As with many cases of police violence, we almost didn't know about George Floyd's 2020 murder on 38th and Chicago in Minneapolis. Reports suggested Floyd died from a medical incident, a story that might not stick out as extraordinary to a busy local reporter. However, Darnella Fraizer's decisions to film the police murder of Floyd and later post the video online were the essential actions that helped the story break.

The history books will catalog the unprecedented sizes of the protests that followed. The mainstream news' coverage of these protests fell in line with past narratives. For example, protester destruction was front and center in much of the *Minneapolis Star Tribune's* coverage. On May 31, 2020, the paper's front-page headline declared, "The Guard moves in" (Louwagie and Condon). The subhead noted that a "Massive deployment aims to quell rioting." A third subhead stated, "Violence convulses cities nationwide over George Floyd's death." Like those initial medical incident reports were countered by Fraizer's video, the mainstream media's story framing was also countered by a piece in *Slate* that would go viral. Matthew Dessem headlined his piece with an entirely different story: "Police Erupt in Violence Nationwide." I credit his article as a critical event that influenced news organizations all over the United States to consider reckoning with racism. Egregious coverage gaffes and journalist staff walkouts helped tip the scales as well.

The marginalization of Black folks and their demands for equality through the press is not isolated and has drastically affected trust. The 1968 Kerner Commission proclaimed that news narratives were constructing "two societies, one Black, one white" and detailed the scandal of how news narratives were used to other, harm, sensationalize, and capitalize on Black people and their pain.

Evidence suggests that most journalists adapt quite quickly to new technologies but cultural shifts and routine changes are the most resistant to change (Eckdale et al. 2015). Such was the case after the commission's damning report. In the 1960s, few convincing reasons that Black people should trust the media were ever spelled out. Since then, few researchers have found mainstream media narratives that better represented Black communities.

As evolving-but-damaging narrative patterns continued for decades, it is of little wonder that trust has been tough to rebuild or acquire in the present day. In late summer 2020, I conducted dozens of interviews with Black news users to see what they thought about the coverage of recent events (Brown, Masullo, and Wilner 2021). Most understood that the mainstream news narratives were incomplete, inaccurate, and misinformed. Many rejected the mainstream altogether. Some were less critical of the news media but shared concerns about how Black people are represented in the news. Trusting in news media was rarely even on the table.

Though mainstream journalism's shortcomings might stifle trust, it has served other functions, like inspiring resistance and innovation inside and outside the newsroom. In some cases, resistance has led to rejecting the mainstream media and pursuing alternative spaces that allow us to plead our own causes. Black Presses, from the *Freedom's Journal's* updates on the abolitionist movement in the 1800s to *The Chicago Defender's* public debates about the welfare of communities in the early 1900s, expanded opportunities for Black voices, perspectives, and stories to be told to others. Today, the Minneapolis/St. Paul metroplex offers a robust and unparalleled network of alternative media spaces that center on Black perspectives and interests. With elite local media like the *Minnesota Spokesman-Recorder*, *Insight News*, and Black Information Network audio news service, such a rich media ecosystem allows many people to avoid the marginalizing outcomes of the mainstream news in its entirety.

However, one of the consistently under-discussed spaces in my work is the role of change agents inside mainstream news institutions. As with most organizations, some agitators and advocates work within mainstream institutions, invested in doing the work it takes to realize change for the better. Past and present, journalism is no stranger to these individuals. In 2020, many newsrooms expanded their leadership teams, placing advocates at the helms of diversity, equity, and inclusion (DEI) initiatives. A little over a week after George Floyd's murder, the *Philadelphia Inquirer* issued an apology (Wischnowski, Escobar, and Kerkstra 2020) for an ill-timed cover story with a front-page banner that featured the importance of property. "Buildings Matter, Too" (Saffron 2020) outraged many, including the paper's employees. The headline was a symptom of a bigger problem, though, and the next day dozens of employees called in sick while also diagnosing the paper's illness in an open letter to the leadership. Protests and petitions were found in major national newspapers, including *The New York Times*, *The Wall Street Journal*, and the *Los Angeles Times*. Editors were called out, and several stepped down from their positions. Organizations started making promises for change.

The New York Times referred to this as a "fallout."

And the reaction to the fallout was unlike what most of us had seen before. Within just a few weeks, many significant changes were made. After decades of advocacy efforts, the B in Black was finally capitalized by many news organizations across the country. We saw an uptick in attention to police violence during protests, a narrative often hidden by passive voice and skewed storytelling. Some newsrooms reviewed their imaging practices and considered the harm of contributing to viral visual accounts of violence against Black people. Newsrooms promised new hires and committed to retention.

DEI initiatives and new editorial positions were created to help manage efforts. At the *Star Tribune*, several people of color were appointed and promoted to upper-level positions, and I met with many to ask them about their challenges and the work ahead. I was curious about journalists and audiences. Who were journalists actually writing for? Newsroom advocate Tom Horgen, who was appointed senior manager of audience strategy in 2016, noted that journalists often weren't thinking about this question. He said that part of the reckoning is convincing the entire newsroom to "actively be thinking about that, the question that you're asking, who are we writing this for? Is the way we're framing the story—the people in the story, the headline—what does that actively say to a community of color?" He continued, "Those are all questions that need to be asked on every single story, and be more intentional about them. And that's the work that I am trying to do to bring that intention and actually ask that question. I want every journalist at the *Star Tribune* when they start the ideation process of a story to ask, who am I writing this for? And every story is going to be different."

Despite recent attention to empowered efforts, there is a long history of this kind of primarily uncelebrated advocacy work in newsrooms. I mention such efforts without attempting to insinuate the mainstream news will now better represent our communities. I have little evidence that recent efforts have dramatically addressed the issue in ways that Black communities might view as reparative. Instead, I mention these efforts as a call for Black communities to look for action and celebrate the wins (albeit small) of those change agents in newsrooms—especially because many of these change agents are members of Black communities.

Kyndell Harkness, who was also promoted to assistant managing editor of diversity and community at the *Star Tribune*, valued community support and positioned it as vital to future progress. "Like ours, a lot of news organizations have had their own sort of reckoning, because they really do need to be upfront and transparent. Like, 'Yeah, we screwed up. We were just like the rest of society; we're racist.' But we also have to say, how are we changing. I think that, when we do that piece, that must be a part of the conversation. Not like, 'Oh, look, here are the things that we have done,' but 'We see where we are, and here's some of the stuff we're going to try and do. We can't do it without you.' Without community being vocal and helping us get better."

During Derek Chauvin's murder trial, I had the opportunity to connect with national reporters as well. One multimedia reporter from a major national news organization allowed me to observe his production process, including the back-and-forth between editors and sometimes-tense conversations about cultural sensitivity in footage. He fought to keep many of the lengthy humanizing narratives in, and he fought to shield his audience from traumatizing images. The final piece did what so many other reports do not in the mainstream: It centered activists' and community members' voices, and it gave deep testimony of victims' lives lived before they were ended by police. In a Twitter Spaces conversation follow-up, one local activist from Minneapolis publicly thanked the journalist and his team.

"Just thank you for telling our story," she said. We can celebrate that progress.

As a researcher who critiques trends, I had rarely taken the time to celebrate trend breakers, a positionality that might offer opportunities to reimagine our relationship with mainstream journalism if we choose. The revolution within is vital to acknowledge, even if mainstream news organizations appear unchanged. Media makers can and are working for change, speaking out about wrongs, and introducing news narratives that might help repair trust. We'll have to look for it, though. We might find it by celebrating the effort of change agents in mainstream institutions as we continue to wait and see if measures can reform news organizations.

References

Brown, Danielle, Gina Masullo, and Tamar Wilner. 2021. "'It's Just Not the Whole Story': Black Perspectives of Protest Portrayals." *Howard Journal of Communications* 33, no. 4: 382–395. https://doi.org/10.1080/10646175.2021.2012852.

Dessem, Matthew. 2020. "Police Erupt in Violence Nationwide." *Slate*, May 31, 2020. https://slate.com/news-and-politics/2020/05/george-floyd-protests-police-violence.html.

Kerner, Otto, chairman. 1968. *Report of the National Advisory Commission on Civil Disorders, i.e. The Kerner Commission.* February 29, 1968. Washington, D.C.

Ekdale, B., Singer, J. B., Tully, M., & Harmsen, S. Making Change: Diffusion of Technological, Relational, and Cultural Innovation in the Newsroom. Journalism & Mass Communication. (2015). *Quarterly*, 92(4), 938-958. https://doi.org/10.1177/1077699015596337.

Louwagie, Pam, and Patrick Condon. 2020. "The Guard moves in: Massive deployment aims to quell rioting: Violence convulses cities nationwide over George Floyd's death." *Minneapolis Star Tribune*, May 31, 2020.

Saffron, Inga. 2020. "Buildings Matter, Too." *The Philadelphia Inquirer*, June 2, 2020.

Wischnowski, Stan, Gabriel Escobar, and Patrick Kerkstra. 2020. "An apology to our readers and Inquirer employees." *The Philadelphia Inquirer*, June 3, 2020. https://www.inquirer.com/news/philadelphia-inquirer-black-lives-matter-headline-apology-20200603.html.

Dr. Danielle K. Brown

Dr. Danielle K. Brown is a social movement and media researcher and holds the 1855 Community and Urban Journalism University Professorship at Michigan State. She is the founding director of the LIFT Project – a project focused on mapping, networking, and resourcing trusted messengers to dismantle dis- and misinformation narratives that circulate in Black communities and about Black communities in other spaces. Danielle consults in newsrooms nationwide to help turn narrative analyses into tools for advancing the profession and encouraging citizen engagement in democracy. Her publicly accessible articles and commentary have appeared in local, national, and international outlets such as *Nature, Scientific American, The Conversation, Columbia Journalism Review, Nieman Lab*, and *The Washington Post*. This work has helped mainstream theories about the protest paradigm and informed the curriculums of training organizations around the country about producing pro-democratic protest reporting. In addition, she has developed workshops and trainings for multiple professional and public audiences, including organizations like the Carnegie Council, Council on Foreign Relations, National Press Club, and the Institute for Journalism & Natural Resources. She has received several early career awards for her efforts, including being honored as the 2024 International Communication Association's Early Career Scholar Award. She previously held the John & Elizabeth Bates Cowles Professorship at the University of Minnesota (2020-2023).

6

Listening for Black Voices

Daniel Pierce Bergin

The newspaper ad is vivid in its simplicity: "*Black Voices* . . . tonight on KTCA." No images. No faces. No logo. Two words conveying the meaning of thousands of words and images.

The *Black Voices* TV series, which ran from 1968 to 1969, was a collaboration between Twin Cities public television (then KTCA/KTCI Channels 2 and 17) and members of the Twin Cities Black community. The title is an apt description of that short-lived conversation program. The title also continues to stand as a call, a directive, for public media to empower and amplify the voices of diverse communities.

Unfortunately, as of 2024, there appear to be no archived recordings of *Black Voices*. "I was told, years ago, actual shows had been recorded over. I truly hope that isn't the case," said Kokayi Ampah, who was involved in the *Black Voices* project as a youth. His fear is well founded. Prior to the digital and server-based media infrastructure of today, it was common practice for TV stations to erase or "wipe" the large-format reel-to-reel videotapes that programs lived on. This practice allowed for budget-saving reuse of the medium, but it also has led to incalculable loss of local history.

Perhaps there is a *Black Voices* recording in the deep archives at the University of Minnesota, a common partner in production in the early days of educational and public TV. Maybe there is an "air check" stored away in the copious collection of recordings of the Paley Center for Media, formerly known as the Museum of Television & Radio, in New York. One can hope. But for now, let us bring *Black Voices* back into being through this invocation.

Like similar social justice programs of the era, *Black Voices* more or less emerged out of the Kerner Commission. In the reckoning following the "riots" that rippled through American cities in the late '60s, President Johnson appointed a think tank led by Illinois governor Otto Kerner. The resulting publication, in 1968, from the commission's work catalyzed a range of endeavors striving for Johnson's "Great Society." Along with recommending increased opportunities for housing, jobs, and education, the commission called out the need for American media to better speak to and with diverse communities who were largely absent from and often assailed by television, radio, and print. So, what had been benignly informative educational TV became something more purposeful to compensate for the "vast wasteland" of American commercial media. This would lead to the birth of the Public Broadcasting Service in 1969.

With a range of funding sources and support levels from a wide variety of local PBS stations, programs for people of color ascended into the airwaves across the country. Some of the programs catering to the African American community, like *Soul!* from WNET and *Like It Is* from WABC, both from New York, are delightfully titled with names capturing the colloquialisms and slang of the era. Other series titles, like *Our People* from WTTW and *For Blacks Only* from KCTV, both from Chicago, are unfiltered expressions of the era's Black Power movement.

In Minnesota, the Indigenous community had an even cooler title. *The Runner* was the proposed name of a series on Native issues. The title calls to mind the traditional messenger in many Native nations who spread news through distance running. Sadly, but not surprisingly, the Native American program seemed to be largely ignored by the funding community as it garnered very little financial support.

With a $75,000 grant from the Rockefeller Foundation, KTCA/KTCI in St. Paul initiated a TV series to feature Black community conversations but also offer training on media production. Kokayi Ampah was a St. Paul Central High School teen who found opportunity and empowerment thanks in part to doting Black leaders and elders: "I became aware that there was a program being put together that was going to teach community people about television production. I was all in. The closest person I knew to the selection committee was Katie McWatt of the Urban League." With connections to elders like McWatt, inspirational community activists-organizers like Bobby Hickman, and organizations like St. Paul's Inner City Youth League and Minneapolis's Phillis Wheatley Center, *Black Voices* seemed well rooted in the community.

As the training sessions got underway, Ampah gained a range of experiences in the KTCA studios, then located on Como Avenue near the Minnesota State Fair grounds. "There was a six-week training program on all the aspects of production: floor directing, camera operation, technical directing, directing, sound, and producing," recalled Ampah, now in his 70s. "I really can't say I felt any hostility from the actual staff. I was too busy lavishing in this opportunity and sucking up all I could. Remember, I was eighteen, just graduated from Central High two weeks before the program began." Following Ampah's training period, the production began. "After the training, we produced hour-long television shows and each week we performed a different task. I learned my strong suits were producing and camera operation."

"Black is beautiful, right? Right." *The Black Voices* premiere in the spring of 1968 caught the eye of *Minneapolis Tribune* entertainment columnist Will Jones. His close watching and glowing response speak to the importance of this non-news self-portraiture from African Americans, even for his presumed white newspaper readers. His article continued:

> The beauty of Blackness is a slogan, a war cry for a particular group of militants in the current struggle to eliminate some of the nonsense from American life. It could also be the logical conclusion of any viewer who happened to tune into the premiere of *Black Voices.*

His overview of the lead episodes provides a solid sense of what the series must have looked, sounded, and *felt* like. At its core was dialogue, conversation, some audience participation, and even edgy, creative tension among the Black panelists. Jones wrote:

In getting started, the premiere hour had some stiff, socially awkward overtones. But once the *Black Voice*s promised by the title began to make themselves heard, the starch came out from the format, and the program just happened.

Not surprisingly, Jones seemed to be looking for conflict and tension, and found it in the premiere's fascinating intergenerational dynamic. "A pair of senior Negro citizens formed a two-man panel to talk about how life was for them hereabouts the turn of the century," wrote Jones. "A larger panel of young Negros came on next to talk about how things are with them today." The elders went on to critique the "violence" of the youth-driven agitation of the late '60s. At that point, according to the review, activist and educator Milt Williams gently challenged the seniors from the audience, saying, "You're beautiful. Your loyalty to your country is beautiful, and you're an example of why Black is beautiful. But because of you, with all due respect, sirs, this is why we're not going to put up with any more." The person making this respectful, radical, eloquent call to action was Milt Williams. *Brother Milt* would become known as elder Mahmoud El-Kati.

Also exciting to consider are what subsequent episodes of *Black Voices* were like. The episodes created by Ampah speak to the series' depth and value. "I produced two shows: 'Religion in the Black Community' and 'Finances in the Black Community,'" recalled Ampah. "I can't remember any censorship by the studio, though that would have been something [producer] Dan [Pothier] would have experienced more than us. My shows were produced just the way I drew them up."

The idea that in 1968 a Black youth from St. Paul could produce hour-long broadcast specials on finances and faith in the Black community takes my breath away. It is also indicative of the program's strength-based narrative. The series seemed to avoid fixation on pathology, pain, and victimhood. Long before we would feel the need to highlight the term *Black Joy,* there was clearly a sense of beauty, hope, and happiness in the community and its storytelling. In fact, the subtitles and descriptions listed in the TV guide of the newspaper show how holistic, sophisticated, and thoughtful the content was. Each episode, it seems, could be equally relevant fifty years later based on these loglines:

"Evolution of R&B," "Medical Needs and Care in the Black Community," "Suburban Blacks," "A Christmas Program featuring choirs from Sabathani, Mt Olivet, and St James churches," "Black Models," "Aviation," "Stillwater Prison," "Unemployment," "The Way's theatre production of sitcom *The Story of Brother Jeroboam*," "Agencies that Serve the Black Community," "Black Youth," "College Students," "Interracial Dating," "Black women's attitudes towards white women."

Of course, salacious subject matter like those last two episodes listed were certain to pique the interest of those outside of the Black community as well. Once again media writer Will Jones tuned in. In his December 1968 review in *The Minneapolis Tribune*, he couldn't get enough of the frank discussion about race and sex featuring notable Black women like Minneapolis Central grad and pioneering lawyer Joyce Hughes.

"Dating Game in Black and White" was his headline. Jones noted that the "women on the panel . . . concentrated on what was bugging them most: the attraction white women seem to have for Black men." He offered several quotes from the panel discussion: "'They don't scare me,' said attorney Joyce Hughes, referring to the blondes. 'Anything they got I got. And I know more.' She was convincing, both audibly and visually," remarked Jones in full-on white male gaze.

His reviews help give us some sense of this (for now) lost TV program. But it is unfortunate that he uses an entire above-the-fold article on the "Jungle Fever" episode and didn't deem episodes about Black college life, pre–Penumbra Black theatre, Black economics, health care, or "aviation" (possibly focused on Black pilots) as worthy of his review. But at least his recounting of this episode shows the dynamism and diversity of Black women leadership in the Twin Cities at that time.

Attempting to moderate the discussion among these strong women was *Black Voices* host and program producer Dan Pothier.

A highly regarded radio DJ for WLOL, Pothier was also a committed community advocate and activist. He was a leader in the Minneapolis Community Protectors street patrols and was involved in a nonlethal shootout with two white men he observed firing gunshots at Plymouth Avenue community fulcrum The Way, where he worked.

Pothier and others attempted to leverage their newly found media prowess into action. They led a call for a boycott of local media outlets that were not hiring Blacks in meaningful numbers or roles.

It is a good thing Pothier and the Black producers sprinted through so much subject matter when they had the chance. The program didn't last long, from 1968 to 1969. Perhaps the funding from Rockefeller was a one-and-done proposition. Perhaps the KTCA staff didn't have the bandwidth to support the project without a sizable infusion of cash from a major foundation. We do know that local foundation support that would drive KTCA to become one of the most active local producers was still a decade away. Whatever the factors, the program was discontinued. Among the personal papers of the late Barbara Cyrus, a participant in the *Black Voices* production, is a 1969 memo from the Black community to KTCA leadership protesting the cancellation of the program. She and the other participants would have to retreat back to the notable but less visible Black Press where many of them came from. Kokayi Ampah recalled the meaningful impact of the program and speculates on what could have been with more *Black Voices*:

> The program aired, as I remember, prime time on Wednesday evening, and it (had) a viewership in the community. People would comment good and bad just like any other show. The community got a chance to raise questions they were thinking of and see their own do it. If it had been allowed to continue, no telling the effect it would have had on coming generations. Some of us did go on to careers in the business or related professions.

That might be the understatement of the century as it relates to his own career. Ampah went on to work in Hollywood in a range of roles and eventually honed his skill in location work, becoming the top location manager for major Hollywood productions. His IMDb list is impressive. His accolades from the film industry are considerable. Now, he works to pass on the opportunities, just as he was nurtured as a youth in St. Paul's vibrant, culturally rich Black community that connected him to opportunities like *Black Voices*.

Ampah, along with SoulTouch Productions executive producer Robin Hickman-Winfield, and the content and uplift they create are descendants from *Black Voices*. Having these media leaders and their work so visible is important, in part, because for a half century the program that helped seed their careers wasn't seen, was lost, other than in their recollections.

Perhaps at the time of your reading this, recordings of *Black Voices* have finally surfaced. If so, I envy you the ability to see these time capsules of Minnesota's Black community. I hope they are lifted up and pointed to—in Sankofa fashion—as beacons of who we were and who we are becoming. But at the time of this writing, one can only imagine the conversations, tone, visual feel, affirmation, and inspiration that must come from watching. This invocation is like that of early astronomers who knew there must be a celestial body because of the tug of its gravity long before it was finally seen. Like archeologists, there were stunning finds beneath the sands of Egypt long before discovering Tutankhamun's gilded tomb.

But regardless of whether the program is ever seen, the sublimity of the title from a half century ago remains an aspirational reminder of the role of public media to lift up Black issues, Black history, Black experience, Black beauty . . . Black voices.

References

Cyrus, Barbara. 1969. Barbara Cyrus Personal Papers Collection. University of Minnesota Library Archive

Jones, Will. 1968. "After Last Night." *Minneapolis Tribune,* May 24, 1968.

Jones, Will. 1968. "Panel Discusses Dating Game in Black and White." *Minneapolis Tribune*, December 15, 1968.

Kerner, Otto, chairman. 1968. *Report of the National Advisory Commission on Civil Disorders, i.e. The Kerner Commission.* February 29, 1968. Washington, D.C.

Daniel Pierce Bergin

Daniel Pierce Bergin creates media that explores diverse people, places, and the past through restorative narratives. The Twin Cities PBS executive producer and WEM Foundation–endowed director has won over twenty regional Emmy Awards for productions ranging from 30-second PSAs to feature-length documentaries, including *Jim Crow of the North*; *Out North: MNLGBTQ History*; *Lost Twin Cities 5*; and *Make It OK: Mental Illness & Stigma*. His documentary *With Impunity: Men and Gender Violence* was named "Best Documentary of 2012" by *Mpls.St. Paul Magazine*. Daniel has had films broadcast across the PBS system and screened at a range of festivals, including Input, the Pan African Film Festival, the Minneapolis St. Paul International Film Festival, the Hollywood Black Film Festival, and the Chicago International Children's Film Festival.

The Minneapolis native and University of Minnesota graduate has served as director on the boards of several community media organizations. Daniel has been an adjunct instructor and lectured and presented in countless schools, colleges, and community settings. He has been recognized as a Minnesota State Arts Board fellow and a *City Pages* Artist of the Year. He received a University of Minnesota Outstanding Alumni Award, an A.P. Anderson Award for significant artistic contributions, and a Bush Leadership Fellowship for his work in community media.

7

Walking in the Footsteps of Uncle Gordon: Keeping the Promise

Dr. Robin P. Hickman-Winfield

This past spring when the invitation came to contribute an essay to this critical and timely collection, I was honored and excited. Then as I attempted to focus on 45-plus years of conscious context creation . . . anxiety gripped me. This essay would be one of the most important representations of my voice, almost sacred. I became overwhelmed, because my community and career journey related to our essay assignment, though extremely blessed, is so broad and even complicated.

After many streams of thoughts and drafts, "The Communicator" just couldn't weave it together. I have so much to say, but what should I say . . . for such a time as this? There are many reasons I needed this piece to be on point, to resonate with folks, and maybe touch souls. Mostly I needed it to be a contribution worthy of the profoundly powerful publication in which it will be presented. Also, worthy of the gracious soul, who again reminded me not to retreat but release the burden. Gratitude. When someone has a soul divinely aligned with your vision, you can trust them to assist in the process of articulating the impact of your calling. I'm grateful.

I'm walking in the footsteps of Gordon Parks as the CEO and executive producer of SoulTouch Productions and establishing my own legacy as a media maker. As a grand-niece and protégé of Gordon Parks, I have been instilled with a lasting legacy of media-making with meaning. My process started early. My mother has a photo of me when I was a baby holding up a copy of his book *The Learning Tree*. I'm in another photo with my grandmother Lillian Parks, Gordon's older sister, right above him, as a baby holding a copy of his book *A Choice of Weapons*. As a twig on the branch of the Parks learning tree, I understand that the legacy is really about the young people. My mother (Patricia), my father (Kofi Bobby), my grandmother (Lillian Parks), my Uncle Gordon, and my beloved village poured into me this love, this legacy, and this life as a child. This was so that I could take my rightful place behind the camera, which is important, and this is where my work has been. I was in love with Uncle Gordon and the work he did. He inspired not only what I'd do for a living but how I'd do it.

Uncle Gordon took a powerful position regarding his media-making and taught me that, as Black people, we have to control the narrative of our people. We do this by being behind the camera and understanding the power of/in it. Uncle Gordon was constantly challenged by the vast issues concerning our community, such as violence, poverty, and racism. Uncle Gordon experienced racism and hardship throughout his youth in Fort Scott, Kansas, his birthplace, and in St. Paul, Minnesota, where he came into manhood. Uncle Gordon highlights these experiences that many Black people, especially men, went through in his first two autobiographies, *The Learning Tree* (1963) and *A Choice of Weapons* (1966). Uncle Gordon, up until his death at the age of 93, felt that not much had improved for Black men in any significant way.

On one of my last visits with Uncle Gordon in New York, before he passed away in 2006, I received my final instructions, my last assignment for my life's work. During that visit, we were talking and, with tears in his eyes, he asked me, **"What's going to happen to Black boys and what did I really do in my life to help them?"** I reminded him of the work that I have been doing in Minnesota pouring his legacy into the lives of young people. I reminded him of my work at Red Wing correctional facility, where he had a connection to the young brothers incarcerated there who were Choice of Weapons Fellows who wrote him letters and each of them had a signed copy of his book *A Choice of Weapons*. I reminded Uncle Gordon that there were hundreds of young people in Minnesota who had read, studied, and discussed his life, his work, and his values. They were using him as a role model, a vision of possibilities; they had now created their own visions of life and acknowledged their own possibilities. So that evening, I promised my uncle that his incredible body of work would not be in vain.

In the work my cousin Anura Si-Asar and I do today, for example, at Gordon Parks High School in St. Paul, where Uncle Gordon lived during his formative years, I tell the students that they are our co–promise keepers. Gordon Parks High, an alternative school with a high representation of youth of color, especially Black young men, has always been surrounded by the Parks family since its inception. In our Choice Fellows program that has been going on for years, we view his movies, we read his books and poetry, we talk about his life and connect it to students' lives today. Students create self-portraits with well-thought-out personal vision statements. A student once asked me, if Uncle Gordon was alive today, what would you tell him? I told her that I would tell him that Black boys will be okay, because they are walking in your footsteps. Thanks to the Choice Fellows program, for the first time Black young men are flying to Fort Scott, Uncle Gordon's birthplace and childhood home, to celebrate his life at the Gordon Parks Museum's annual celebration. There, students take part in critical discussions about Uncle Gordon's work and legacy. Students are meeting other artists who Uncle Gordon inspired, like Kyle Johnson who starred in the 1969 film version of *The Learning Tree*, Roger E. Mosley who starred in the film *Leadbelly*, and David Parks, Uncle Gordon's son. For the first time, Black young men are visiting New York, where Uncle Gordon spent much of his adult life, to visit the annual Gordon Parks Foundation Awards Dinner, where Black young men have the opportunity to meet some of their role models like rapper Black Thought from *The Tonight Show*, the late great Congressman John Lewis, and author Ta-Nehisi Coates, a Gordon Parks Foundation honoree. Again, I would tell my uncle that Black boys will be alright.

Our youth will be alright because we brought David Parks to Gordon Parks High's 10th Anniversary Celebration, the National Black Journalist Conference, and the Walker Art Center so that students could listen to and walk with the man who walked with the man, Gordon Parks. Students connect to the Parks family, who carry on Uncle Gordon's legacy in multifaceted ways. This is a transformative movement. The media legacy work we do with our students is designed to armor them up, so if they find themselves in an adverse situation, they can use their choice of weapons to deal with it. We must armor up our children and our community. The process of knowledge-based transformation in our young people's lives is the key to our freedom. Exposing students to role models who can connect to their lives is critical. Role models who look like them, and who have been through some of the same things they have, is of utmost importance. We have brought in actor Richard Roundtree, actor/producer Robert Townsend, acclaimed photographer Jamel Shabazz, and many others to speak life into our youth. Multimedia is the key to reach our youth. One of the best examples of a person addressing life, love, legacy, and social issues is none other than the Renaissance man himself, Gordon Parks, who used many powerful mediums to do this.

The Lovin' the Skin I'm In Sisters at Gordon Parks High had the opportunity to partner with Frank Murphy's fashion store to recreate the fashion photographs that first made Uncle Gordon famous. It was at Frank Murphy's in 1940 where Uncle Gordon had the courage to ask the owner if he could photograph the models, which in turn launched Uncle Gordon's career in fashion photography. The young ladies of Gordon Parks High honored his legacy in such a beautiful way with their photographs. They learned about perseverance when Uncle Gordon double-exposed all the photographs of his photoshoot with Frank Murphy's models, except one. And with that one photograph, Frank Murphy saw the talent, artistry, and potential of this young Black man and gave him another shot at the photoshoot. The ladies then crossed the street to the luxurious historic Saint Paul Hotel, where Uncle Gordon had worked as a busboy and waiter in his youth, to take their own stunning high-fashion photographs.

Uncle Gordon is known for breaking the color barrier in many artistic and journalistic fields. In 1969, he directed, wrote the screenplay and the musical score for, and produced *The Learning Tree*, a movie about his early life in Kansas. Uncle Gordon understood, as the first Black director in Hollywood, that he had to bring others with him and change practices not just in front of his camera but behind it too. As Uncle Gordon put it, "A multitude of hopeful young Black directors would be watching, counting on me to successfully open those closed doors" and "could think, at least, it's possible." As my cousin David Parks points out on the making of *Shaft*, "There were a lot of Black actors, a lot of Black crew that were brought in on the set to be able to get them qualified as production people for the unions. Black electricians and production assistants and stuff. He got a lot of people in there and as well as my brother [Gordon Parks Jr]. He brought in some younger people and got them into the industry."

Susan Robeson (the granddaughter of Paul Robeson) and I cofounded and were executive producers of *Don't Believe the Hype*. This show was directly modeled after Uncle Gordon's philosophy of ensuring Black people are included in the narrative, image, and production of film. This Twin Cities Public Television TPT/PBS (KTCA) program aired from 1993 to 2003, with youth of color as the stars and producers of their own productions. Students would learn media production skills, produce original projects of their own, and learn about Uncle Gordon's work and legacy at the same time. I tell my students all the time that I went through the same process as them learning about myself and my community. I learned from Uncle Gordon and his nephew, my father, Bobby Hickman, who was the director of Inner-City Youth League, which operated a media arts program like *Hype* and a Choice Fellows program that taught young people about the importance of being in front of and behind the cameras with consciousness of who they are. As an attempt to "remedy" the racial unrest of the '60s, public television had been mandated to support the development and distribution of programming produced by communities of color. *Black Voices*, a studio-based public affairs show that aired from 1968 to 1969, presented the issues and culture of the Twin Cities Black community. As a young girl, my exposure to seeing Black people in front of, and behind the camera, provided a vision of possibilities. In 2020, I returned to TPT/PBS and reinstituted *Don't Believe the Hype*, continuing its commitment to engage young people of color in legacy learning, community engagement, and producing positive narratives.

Without this type of mentorship, process programming, and commitment from the community, I would not have been an executive producer at Twin Cities Public Television, assistant location manager and community outreach coordinator for HBO's television miniseries *Laurel Avenue* (1993), or producer on *Half Past Autumn: The Life and Works of Gordon Park*s

(2000). I would not have fulfilled my vision of being the CEO and executive producer of SoulTouch Productions, my own business.

Uncle Gordon's legacy, my legacy, is about the legacy we leave to our youth. As Uncle Gordon wrote in *Half Past Autumn: A Retrospective* (1997), "Finally, after a long search to find weapons to fight off the oppression of my adolescence, I found two powerful ones, the camera, and the pen." He also stated that, although "Racism is still around, I am not about to let it destroy me." Uncle Gordon affirmed his message to the *Hype* crew in 1996 when he visited St. Paul and told them that "Media power is Black power" and that he expects much more from them than himself, because this generation is much brighter.

References

Parks, Gordon. 1963. *The Learning Tree*. New York: Harper & Row

Parks, Gordon. 1966. *A Choice of Weapons*. New York: Harper & Row.

Parks, Gordon, director. 1969. *The Learning Tree* (film). Warner Bros.

Parks, Gordon. 1997. *Half Past Autumn: A Retrospective*. Boston: Bulfinch.

Dr. Robin P. Hickman-Winfield

Dr. Robin P. Hickman-Winfield is the CEO and executive producer of SoulTouch Productions, a television and film production, youth development, and community engagement consulting company, with a mission to make meaningful media and produce powerful social impact experiences. Robin was the director of Taking Our Place Centerstage (TOPC) and organizational strategist at the Ordway Center for the Performing Arts. TOPC engaged and partnered with members of Indigenous, Latino, Asian, and Black communities to bring nationally recognized talent to the Ordway and engage local communities with them. She helped produce with VocalEssence a production of *WITNESS: Honoring the Life and Legacy of Gordon Parks* at the Ordway. Robin is the founder and creative director/artist at A Celebration of Soulful Dolls, an inspiring doll artistry that uniquely presents positive and powerful imagery of family, community, and history, with a splash of social commentary! Robin with other Parks family members works with Gordon Parks High School in St. Paul on the Gordon Parks Legacy Educational Experience, which engages students in understanding their vision, purpose, and possibilities. As the great-niece of Gordon Parks, she instills his legacy in all the work she does.

8

Storytelling: More than a Defense Mechanism

Jasmine Snow

I knew what I was getting myself into—or, at least, I thought I did.

At the very least, I knew the stats.

I knew, in the years when I had decided reporting was what I wanted to do, that trust in the media was nearing the lowest it had ever been. I knew the communities I wanted to show up for trusted and were served by the media even less than that. I knew I would have to be working against relentless campaigns of mis- and disinformation that even the most seasoned professionals were bending under.

But it was a fight I felt ready for and I couldn't wait to get started.

I can't imagine that growing up as a mixed person of color in rural South Dakota is anyone's dream. It wasn't mine, at the outset or now—separate from the boundless love I have for both sides of my family. Growing up in a predominantly white area meant having my own experiences with and indignation against discrimination, inequality, and everything else I was noticing in the world discounted or deemed hysterical. It put me at a personal DEFCON 1, constantly feeling like I had to know everything, *be* everything.

I coped with this by *burning* through whatever knowledge I could get my hands on. In middle school, I graduated from my arsenal of simple library books on American history and Black cultural movements to hardcore journalism. I felt like I had to be ready for some kind of battle almost every day, and I knew I needed something more substantive than *my feelings* and quicker than pseudo-academic tapestries to make it through unscathed (or, in this case, respected as a thinking person). This pressure invariably affected what news I consumed and the way I consumed it. Most of my free time was spent with the news: endless scrolling through *CNN, The Washington Post, The New York Times, Reuters, Bloomberg, Fox, Time, The Wall Street Journal* . . . I read any article within thumbs reach, something I now know to be Sisyphean and fraught in the age of the 24-hour news cycle and toxic Twitter trending lists.

Back then, all I could think was: If I wasn't using my privilege of time and access to resources, what good was I to anyone? As I got older, I got angrier. The headlines hit closer and closer to home, and so many people around me seemed to be carrying on unaffected. I felt corralled, often, into defending the right to choose and affirmative action. I felt like I had to know the names and details of every Black person murdered by the police for the next time someone inevitably brought it up *just in case*. It was as if it was my personal responsibility to pick up every gauntlet that had been thrown down in my general vicinity. I railed, raged—vocally and often. It did little good.

But somewhere along the way—between all the tripe and the tragedy—I learned storytelling could be more than a defense mechanism. After the death of my niece, I dove headfirst into memoirs about grief and personal essays on loss. My senior year, I qualified for the National Speech and Debate Association competition with a piece about the health effects of racism on Black women. I learned, almost all at once, that I had never been alone in feeling so helpless and outraged and *responsible*. More than any of that, I learned that affirmations of reality didn't always have to be a shield or a weapon. Stories could be more than things I used to protect myself or strike down others.

After that, I struggled to see storytelling as anything else than *what I was meant to do*.

An onus or a privilege, it didn't matter—I felt it was my duty to tell the stories I had always felt I was missing from, if only for the off chance that it might help someone else from feeling the same way I did. I had always been a writer, and I had cultivated words and knowledge as my specialty.

Now, I wanted to be *of use*. And so: journalism.

I came to the University of Minnesota in 2019 with all sorts of stories to tell and people to show up for. I started at *The Minnesota Daily*, our campus paper, as the national headlines reporter on city desk, and I set to work. I actively engaged in discussions regarding how we were (or, most often and historically, *weren't*) serving our community through diverse and equitable coverage. Soon, I joined the Content Diversity Board, where we tried to translate those conversations into action: coverage guides, source wrangling, outreach, trainings, workshops. COVID-19 sent us home, and the murder of George Floyd and subsequent uprisings pulled the floor out from under us.

It took me a while to realize I was running on fumes. Really, I had come into this all armed with very little other than blind optimism and a secret belief that people, once they were truly, *thoroughly* informed, would stop believing in the same beliefs that had hurt me all these years. Arrogance or hope, a secret part of me really thought that systems (the city, the university, student groups) did harmful things, in part, because they were *unaware*. I thought being a journalist meant I could single-handedly spread that awareness and ensure a better path forward.

Thankfully, I've since been taken down a few pegs.

The thing is: It is a scary time to be coming into this industry. Almost every early-career journalist of color I know—my friends, people I've worked with, those I follow on social media—has thought about or begun sharpening their spoons to dig their way up and out. We've spent the last few years sidelined by a public health crisis and subsequent states of lockdown. Experiencing devastation after devastation in our communities has burnt out even the brightest of us, and the constant threat of unemployment looms over those who remain. In 2022 alone, we've watched giants like Gannett and CNN bend and break under the weight of layoffs and dissolution, not to mention the folding hordes of smaller, local outlets across the country. We've seen our friends, peers, mentors, and heroes be pushed to the brink (and sometimes over it) with little more than a *how do you do* from this machine we have all dedicated so much to.

Pandemic aside, it isn't as if issues like this are wholly novel. There are arguments to be made that journalism has been on a downswing for years now and recent events have simply shed light on existing cracks. Of course the pandemic combined with the protests and uprisings in 2020 *were* huge parts of how we got to where we are now. Working in this industry during such a time of isolation, constant trauma, and chaos hasn't been easy on anyone, let alone those of us just showing up to the party looking to learn and grow.

But I still think there's so much I, and other early-career journalists, have to look forward to in starting our journeys now.

For all the financial struggle and insecurity, you can find just as many mentors and connections who will ferret out paid opportunities and other resources. I've heard horror stories of the old school: reporters stampeding from scoop to scoop and willing to put out someone's eye if asked for a double byline. That's not to say competition in the industry is dead or that territorial reporters are extinct, nor is it to say some of this behavior wasn't or still isn't warranted. (Especially considering many of the reporters who were most often trampled over and erased were BIPOC—*especially* women of color.)

However, with some exceptions, there seems to have been at least some healthy shift between then and now. From my experience, if you're willing to put the time in and suffer the odd soft-rejection, a never-ending line of people is willing to go to the mat to ensure you are best equipped to head out into the field. If you're a young journalist of color looking for footing, you don't have to look far for contacts to put in a good word for you at their publication or complete strangers willing to buy you coffee and dispense wisdom on a random Friday afternoon. I know I've done nothing by myself. I am eternally grateful to all of the professors, editors, reporters, activists, and sources who've helped me when I needed it the most. Every door I've walked through so far in journalism—like freelancing for the *Minnesota Spokesman-Recorder* or an internship at the *Minneapolis Star Tribune*—was wrenched open by an elder who was willing to take a chance on me.

It may not be sunshine and rainbows, but we're not going to be left out in the cold.

There is still the issue of what we're being brought into, of course. While the outset does sometimes look bleak, there seem to be shifts in the sort of honesty and care current journalists and industry vets are adopting as standard practice. For example, watching the slow death of the "objectivity" standard in mainstream media has been a special joy of mine. Some choose to cling to the idea of it; some (scholars, writers at *The Objective*, etc.) have rededicated portions of their career to chronicle all the ways it never existed in the first place. It's a fight early-career journalists still partake in, if only in passing. Our realities seem largely centered with a sentiment much closer to, "Okay, fine, you can't be objective. What next?" and I, for one, couldn't be happier.

I am particularly glad to watch the strides taken in discussions of mental health and journalism. This kind of discourse is certainly not unique to journalism but, in an industry where burnout, depression, anxiety, and post-traumatic stress disorder play such a huge role in who stays and who can't, it is *important*. Thankfully, acknowledging journalists' mental health seems like something a majority of us who have the time, privilege, and resources to talk about it can agree on. There is still some lingering romanticization of days-gone-by and some sentiment from certain old-school diehards that we ought to tough it out quietly and at the end of the workday. But I am glad that ongoing, serious conversations are happening about leaving space to take care of ourselves emotionally, as well as professionally. I am most grateful to my Black mentors who have always kept it real with me regarding their own struggles with mental health, trauma porn in storytelling, and their sense of obligation to our community.

Still, we are in the business of skepticism. Journalism is a power structure, and no matter our intentions, it is always important to question where we are, how we got here, and where we're going. It's not my intention to rain down undue praise or sell this industry as something it's not. I just got here—I'm wholly skeptical of the kinds of journalists these last few years have produced and managers' commitment to see change through to the end. There are surely places where we've been overpromised and where accountability has fallen through the cracks.

Considering that, I still believe real change has happened across academic spaces, community spaces, and newsrooms and that more, better change is still coming.

What I've found being young and Black in the media now is that it's all about standing on shoulders and sharing the soup in the pot. It's about honoring those who opened doors for you by going through them, and making sure other people can pass through more easily after you're gone. Those who are able to stick it out have such fertile (if imperfect) ground to sow. That is not to say we are inherently the best equipped to do so. But I don't think we've been so outfoxed that we can't try. It's undeniable that *some* change has definitely happened. For better or worse, I think there is room for us to have a real, fighting chance to leave this place a bit better than we found it.

Really, all I've ever wanted to do was show up for *my people*, whoever that is. That meant more to me than just throwing Black stories against white backdrops and waiting to see what would stick. I wanted to tell stories about rural health access and advocacy groups and farmers. I wanted to tell stories about how communities come together and why they fall apart. I wanted to tell stories about Black hair and racism in medicine. I wanted to tell nerdy Black girl stories. I wanted to tell stories that did some good. I like to think I've begun chipping away at that goal by now, but I know I have the tools somewhere to try again soon.

I used to think of journalism as the way I took the world down a size. It was a way I could take something so big and so scary and make it fit comfortably in the palm of my hand. But now I understand it as this great big *thing* that I love so dearly. Something that should be used to help and heal and hold us all to the mark.

For all my naivete and wrong-footedness, I don't think I'm so off base.

So, if you feel called, come on in. Stay as long as you like and leave if you have to. Take a breath and be willing to learn—everybody's been where you are, and most will want to help get you someplace better. Be humble and kind, and the rest should sort itself out. Someone will be with you shortly. Take care.

Jasmine Snow

Jasmine Snow is a storyteller, a journalist, a researcher, and a craft enthusiast. She is passionate about community-centered work and believes that nothing is possible without working for and alongside the communities she belongs to and lives with. Originally from South Dakota, she's been steadily heading east, collecting an undergraduate degree from the University of Minnesota and currently working on a master's in journalism at Michigan State University. Her work has been featured in places like *The Minnesota Star Tribune*, the *Sahan Journal*, *The Minnesota Daily*, the *Minnesota Spokesman-Recorder*, and the University of Minnesota's *The Tower* literary art magazine.

9

Duluth, Minnesota, at a Crossroads: Solutions for Becoming a Beloved Community of the North

Henry Banks

Duluth, Minnesota, is *at a crossroads*. Our African Heritage community is growing, and it's grieving too. African Heritage individuals and families are moving here for a better quality of life. A quality of life that allows them to breathe in peace and raise a healthy family in a relatively safe and carefree environment. Yet Duluth remains *at a crossroads*. African Heritage individuals are not moving here to cause death and destruction, nor are they here to commit crimes, as they are often accused of doing by city residents. The main perpetrators of death and destruction and incidents of crime are generally and almost exclusively the largest population group in the community. In this case, it is the white population that is causing the majority of problems in our city. Statistics on crime bear witness to this.

At the time of the 2020 United States Census, the African Heritage population in Duluth was 2,057. That's approximately 2.4 percent of the overall population of 86,697 residents residents (US Census Bureau 2020). The census also concluded that the African Heritage population in Duluth experienced the largest increase in population growth of any group. Yet Duluth remains *at a crossroads*.

In comparison, according to the 2020 census, St. Cloud, Minnesota (total population 68,462), had an African Heritage population of 5,152, or 7.5 percent of the overall population. Mankato, Minnesota (total population 44,488), had an African Heritage population of 2,653, or 6 percent of the overall population. Moorhead, Minnesota (total population 44,505), had an African Heritage population of 2,225, or 5 percent of overall population. Like Duluth these are smaller, rural, outstate Minnesota cities with a growing African Heritage population and a history of racial inequities. Strikingly, all of these communities are significantly smaller in overall population than Duluth, but have a larger percentage of African Heritage people.

According to Minnesota Department of Employment and Economic Development data, the unemployment rate for Duluth is *at a crossroads*. The statistics show, pre-pandemic, that African Heritage individuals in Duluth were at approximately 20 percent unemployment (White 2016). That's amongst the highest in the state.

Of the 1,500 individuals on an affordable housing waiting list in Duluth, approximately 15 percent are African Heritage, even though we are only 2.4 percent of the overall population in Duluth and only 1.6 percent of the population in St. Louis County. The prospects for African Heritage individuals to attain a home in Duluth are abysmal. According to Stacker, the 2020 overall homeownership rate of African Heritage people in Duluth is 44 percent. In contrast, the homeownership rate for whites in Duluth is 75 percent. The homeownership rate for African Heritage individuals in Duluth is amongst the worst in the nation. According to a St. Louis County Continuum of Care report in 2022, African Heritage and other persons of color make up 8 percent of people in the county, 18 percent of people in poverty, 39 percent of people who are unsheltered, and 42 percent of people in the county's homeless programs. These numbers are in stark contrast to the overall statistics of St. Louis County, which shows vividly that the African Heritage population continues to experience exacerbated economic, educational, health, and social disparities. Duluth, as the largest city in the county, remains *at a crossroads*.

Duluth Public Schools, which are collectively known as Independent School District 709 or ISD 709, had a high school graduation rate in 2022 for our African Heritage students of a mere 41 percent. The same year, the graduation rate of white students was 83 percent. Duluth remains *at a crossroads*.

Police interactions with our African Heritage students in ISD 709 have gone from bad to worse. A report released on April 5, 2022, by the Law Enforcement Accountability Network (LEAN) Duluth showed glaring racial disparities in the citations issued by police to students of color. These disparities have received significant publicity. In addition to media attention and responses from officials at the Duluth Police Department, the City of Duluth, and ISD 709, LEAN Duluth has received feedback from the African Heritage community about this continuing and alarming law enforcement problem in our city:

> Over and over again, ISD 709's disciplinary measures have proven to be disparately punitive depending on the race of the student. The data shows that ISD 709 refers Black [African Heritage] students to law enforcement at disproportionate levels when compared to their white colleagues, making them increasingly vulnerable to continued conflict, punishment, and trauma. In the *Duluth News Tribune's* April 10th, 2022 article (Bowen 2022) Ebony Hilman, co-chair of the Duluth Branch NAACP's Education Committee, said, "We think that there should be alternatives to School Resource Officers in schools . . . SROs cause more citations and add to the school-to-prison pipeline." However, the article also includes comments from Assistant Superintendent Anthony Bonds adding:
>
> *We have some serious concerns articulated by certain segments of our community, and we also have another segment of our community saying their experiences have been pleasant and they support [it]. So, we're in a predicament where we have to make a decision on what we believe is best for all.*
>
> There is a need to re-think how conflict in schools is handled, not only after it has occurred but with an eye to prevention as well. What other options can be used before police intervention becomes necessary? Most notably, why is it that an escalation to police intervention happens more frequently for Black [African Heritage] children? (LEAN Duluth 2022)

After the damning report was released, ISD 709 turned to community members for discussion and solutions. The school district hosted a comprehensive strategic planning meeting on May 16, 2022, at the American Indian Community Housing Organization, with dinner and childcare provided. ISD asked attendees to help brainstorm ideas for changing the system and bettering the outcomes for Duluth students of color. After the meeting, Classie Dudley, Duluth branch NAACP president, said:

> Turnout was high at this event, especially for the BIPOC community. People spoke up, especially against cops in the schools. We are now left wondering, "Did they hear us? We turned out and spoke up, but what will ISD 709 do now that they know what we want?" I hope that the BIPOC community, whose kids are most negatively affected by these policies, are valued when determining these next steps. (LEAN Duluth 2022)

Duluth and the state of Minnesota, we can and should fix these persistent problems as they continue to negatively impact our African Heritage population. If nothing else, let's fix these problems for our children. After all is said and done, it's about their future.

Immediate Solutions

1. It is imperative that the City of Duluth move forward with a plan to build sustainable infrastructure for its small African Heritage community. Every African Heritage woman, man, and child in Duluth must be given free and equitable housing and must be given, at minimum, a $600 monthly stipend in the form of reparations. The Duluth legacy of the 1920 lynchings of Elias Clayton, Elmer Jackson, and Isaac McGhie has had and will continue to have an impact on the African Heritage community of Duluth. The stipend must last in perpetuity.

2. It is imperative that ISD 709 implement and fully support an academic curriculum that brings to the forefront the attainments of prominent African Heritage leaders of the past and now, and they must prepare themselves for implementation of a fully budgeted and designed educational program focused solely on the African Heritage diaspora. Our children deserve to know where they came from and the greatness that exists in our community. Staffing for this program must be exclusively from the African Heritage community. It would cost approximately $475,000 to $500,000 per year to implement and sustain this important educational program. The figure was suggested by local African Heritage leaders in Duluth at meetings held in City Hall between 2018 and 2020.

3. The need for space and place—to call our own, to self-actualize, to learn, to grow as African Heritage people in a predominantly white environment. The initial price for such a facility: $10 million. This price was suggested by those same leaders at Duluth African Heritage Hub meetings at City Hall between 2018 and 2020.

Besides those three big solutions, there are many possible solutions that can be executed on a smaller scale. I personally have contributed to creating a space for people of African Heritage by creating the radio program *People of Color with Henry Banks*. The program ran from 2011 to 2019. It was broadcast in northwest Wisconsin, northeastern Minnesota, and the Upper Peninsula of Michigan.

My motivation for creating the radio show was to share with a wider audience the successes and contributions made by African Heritage and BIPOC individuals. My goal was to share it with the Twin Ports area of Duluth, Minnesota, and Superior, Wisconsin. I had heard from so many people in the community that issues of importance were not being elevated by local mainstream media in this region. So I wanted to do something to elevate the concerns that people in the community were bringing forward to me and find solutions to those concerns.

When I first came up with my idea for *People of Color*, I called the regional general manager of Wisconsin Public Radio to request a meeting to discuss something that would be really important for their radio station to consider. The meeting took place with the regional general manager, the news director of the region, and one of their producers. All three of them sat on one side of the table, and I sat alone on the other. I flipped the script and started interviewing them. By the end of the interview, they saw the importance of the show and gave me a slot during drive time and wanted it live. This was a prime-time slot that everyone with a talk show would want. I'm still amazed by the timeslot *People of Color* got and, to this day, I don't know why the radio executives gave me such a good spot. My program played Thursdays at 6 p.m. on 91.3 FM KUWS and 90.9 WUWS. They even brought on the producer to help with the production side of things.

People of Color had a simple formula. It was an hour-long program where listeners got to learn about an interesting topic through diverse voices and thoughts. I spent a lot of energy each week choosing a topic, researching it, choosing guests or professionals, developing questions necessary for holistic conversations, and, most importantly, making sure solutions were always part of the conversation. I would get all that material ready a week or two ahead of time and always made sure a backup show was ready to go if the guest speaker was a no-show or couldn't make it.

Though *People of Color* was based in Duluth, our guests weren't just from here. We had regional guests from Superior and northwest Wisconsin, from Minneapolis and St. Paul, and we had national guests from all across the United States and even international guests. It really depended on the topic I wanted to have discussed. I worked hard to find different perspectives and have even gone as far as inviting members of the Ku Klux Klan on to the show. I wanted to bring people on with varying perspectives and opinions; that way, I could give us a chance to challenge ourselves. That alone gave us our credibility. If we want to grow as a society, we need to listen to all types of perspectives.

Because of the radio program, perspectives on the Black community changed. People would literally come up to me in the streets to tell me about the shift in their thinking. It was rewarding to hear how avid listeners had their perspectives changed because of different interviews and guest speakers. The program was absolutely expanding the horizons of the listeners. A lot of them were Caucasian and had their life changed by some of the topics discussed on the show.

The program enriched the Twin Ports area by featuring topics that not only resonated with the African Heritage community but also the Native, Latino, and Asian communities, while at the same time providing a mechanism to the wider audience about our growth in this region and how our growth has had and will continue to have a positive impact on this region. The program reached a lot of white people who lived in remote areas, individuals who otherwise would not get the pertinent information they would need about our growth and contributions to this part of the country. So it had that impact. *People of Color* was the only program of its type in all of Wisconsin, which really says something about the area we are living in.

I'm very happy with what the folks who worked on the show and I accomplished during its eight-year period. I volunteered a lot of my efforts and time to the show. I feel very accomplished for that because it really made a difference.

People of Color ended in 2019 and is not being shared as it should because it is not made available to the public. The past couple of years, I have been contemplating how to reestablish the program, and how to continue delving into issues of importance for people of African Heritage in the Twin Ports. My goal is to bring *People of Color with Henry Banks* back in podcast form and use other tools and forms of communication to get that information to an even larger audience nationwide but also focusing on remote areas that otherwise don't get this information. I know other people want this too. What I attempt to do with my shows is find factual information and candid speakers. I make sure speakers bring solutions to the issues we talk about. It's very important to be solution based. I strongly believe that.

From what I have seen, there are no current entities doing what *People of Color* did. The Native community has their own radio shows that have been happening for decades now. We don't have that in the Black community.

Duluth is *at a crossroads*. A decision must be made. Will we accept local media that ignores the issues that are important to African Heritage people or, worse, that portrays us as perpetrators of death and destruction? Will we accept an African Heritage high school graduation rate of 41 percent in our city? A school-to-prison pipeline hastened by disparately punitive School Resource Officers? An educational system that ignores the contributions of Black leaders? A BIPOC poverty rate of 18 percent? An unemployment rate of 20 percent? An unsheltered rate of 39 percent?

Will we listen to the African Heritage community's ideas about how to change police–student interactions in our public schools? Will we invest in a facility for the African Heritage people of Duluth to call our own? Will we provide the housing and stipends necessary to help repair the historical violence and oppression committed against African Heritage people in Duluth? Will we fund educational programs that lift up the African Heritage diaspora and educate our children about the greatness of African Heritage leaders past and present? Will we produce African Heritage–led media in the form of podcasts, radio, and digital and print journalism—media that speaks to the issues facing the BIPOC community as well as expands the horizons of white listeners? Most importantly, will we make sure solutions are always part of the conversation?

References

Bowen, Joe. 2022. "Duluth school district considers changes to police contract." *Duluth News Tribune*, April 10, 2022. https://www.duluthnewstribune.com/news/local/duluth-school-district-considers-changes-to-police-contract.

Duluth Public Schools. 2022. "Duluth Public Schools graduation rates increase." www.isd709.org/about-us/district-news/news-details/~board/duluth-public-schools-news/post/duluth-public-schools-graduation-rates-increase.

LEAN Duluth. 2022. Racial Disparities Are Evident in Citations Issued to Students at Independent School District 709 in Duluth, MN [report], April 5, 2022. www.leanduluth.org/school-to-prison-pipeline.

St Louis County. 2022. St Louis County Continuum of Care Annual Report. https://www.stlouiscountymn.gov/Portals/0/Library/Dept/Public%20Health%20and%20Human%20Services/Divisions/Homeless/2022%20Annual%20Report.pdf?ver=gtXOkjxJ2GsFvOCuEplGFw%3d%3d.

Stacker. 2022. "The Black Homeownership Gap in Duluth." March 22, 2022. https://stacker.com/minnesota/duluth/black-homeownership-gap-duluth.

US Census Bureau. 2020. "Minnesota." https://data.census.gov/profile/Minnesota?g=040XX00US27.

White, Erik. 2016. "Silver Linings in Northeast Minnesota: Where We Are and the Road Ahead."

White, Erik. 2016. "Silver Linings in Northeast Minnesota: Where We Are and the Road Ahead." Minnesota Department of Employment and Economic Development, January 2016. https://mn.gov/deed/newscenter/publications/review/january-2016/silver-linngs.jsp.

Henry Banks

Born and liberally raised with conservative values in St. Joseph, Missouri, Henry Banks is a child of God, a community activist, a closeted glory seeker, and a nobleman. During his bronze years, he championed his way through academia—graduating from the University of Minnesota and brilliantly securing a degree in political science. It was not long before Banks penetrated the professional arena. Eventually thrusting himself into the multilayered position of executive producer, program author, coordinator, and department head of the African American Student Services Program, Banks grew to become a bushwhacker for African Heritage folk living in Duluth, Minnesota. During his golden years, Banks took on a new inspiration that led him to register for the running of Duluth City Council under the banner "Banks for Duluth." Though he was able to capture 18 percent of the public's vote, he was gently let down in defeat by his opponent. Banks was the first African American man to serve on the ISD 709 school board. He was elected on November 29, 2023. Henry Banks is the founder and first chair of the Clayton Jackson McGhie Memorial in Duluth. These days, in his silver years, Banks spends a considerable portion of his downtime channeling through thrift store aisles in search of humble acquisitions. Banks is currently working on his first book, to be published in the coming years.

10

Minnesota Spokesman-Recorder: **A Family Legacy**

Tracey L. Williams-Dillard

The *Minnesota Spokesman-Recorder* (MSR) is the oldest African American business in Minnesota, a Black family–owned newspaper. We are 90 years old—celebrating 90 years of Black journalistic excellence. It is also one of the oldest Black periodicals in the country still run by a family. Many Black newspapers still in existence today have switched hands. They've been bought out by bigger conglomerates, or someone else bought the paper and the original family doesn't own it anymore. The Black Press not only speaks about our current times but preserves our collective community memory. This collective memory is critical to our identity as a people and a community. MSR is a model for institution building, a beacon of hope, and a vision of possibilities for our community.

As the current CEO and publisher of the *Minnesota Spokesman-Recorder*, I did not always see myself in the newspaper business. My story is one of transformation and direct preparation by my grandfather, grandmother, mother, and other family members. My story begins in Des Moines, Iowa, where I was born to teen parents, who had also been born and raised in Iowa. My biological grandfather Wallace Jackman Sr. was a hard worker who always had two or more jobs. One of his jobs was auto mechanic. He had personal challenges that led my grandmother, Launa Quincy, to divorce him. My grandmother left Iowa in 1960 with my mother, Norma Jean, for better opportunities in Minnesota. They moved to South Minneapolis.

In Minneapolis, there were five of us who grew up together. From the oldest to the youngest, there is Vicky, me (Tracey), Jimmy, Greg, and Tina. I also have stepsiblings, Oscar and Joyce. Being raised in South Minneapolis, you were either a 38th Street person or a 46th Street person, and I was a 46th

Street girl. I went to Field Elementary School, Ramsey Junior High, and Washburn High.

My grandmother remarried in 1965 to a newspaper publisher named Cecil Newman. He was the publisher of the *St. Paul Recorder* and the *Minneapolis Spokesman*. When she met and married my grandfather, she offered to help him run the paper. He declined. But my grandmother was a doer and a force to be reckoned with, and soon after, she integrated herself into his newspaper business, becoming invaluable. She didn't have any problems pulling up her sleeves and jumping right in and helping wherever she could. My grandmother raised her two children: my mother, Norma, and my uncle, Wallace Jackman Jr. They both helped and learned about the family publishing business. Of course, the grandchildren also got involved at a very early age. Vicky, being the oldest, initially took on many roles at the paper, but she didn't like it much. I enjoyed learning and helping with many different tasks.

All of us were readers of the Black Press. My grandmother had Black periodicals sitting on the table from all around the country. We loved and admired our grandmother, and we wanted to know what she was reading, not just the *Spokesman* and the *Recorder*. We understood as young people how important Black media was, at least intuitively, although none of the grandchildren initially thought we would carry on the family's publishing tradition.

My Grandfather—Cecil Newman

Mr. Cecil Newman, my grandfather, was born in 1903 in Kansas City, Missouri. His dream of being a journalist started in the eighth grade. He wrote for his school newspaper, and he loved history. Back in the early 1900s, much of the educational system prepared Black boys for manual labor jobs. My grandfather wanted a career. So for him to have a vision, to want to be a newspaper journalist at such a young age and then follow his dream, was a significant feat. Even though he had several jobs as a teen—delivering newspapers, running a concession stand at a movie theater, doing carpentry work—in his heart he was an entrepreneur. He even bought a semipro baseball team and managed it, as a teenager.

During the time my grandfather grew up in Kansas City, it was segregated. It may not have been as bad as the deep South, but segregation was segregation. His daily life was severely impacted by the evil of segregation. In 1919, when my grandfather was 16 years old, the Black newspaper *The Call* was founded in Kansas City. He got a job there while in high school doing various things. He even wrote for them. *The Call* was an activist paper that challenged segregation and the mistreatment of African Americans, and it told the stories of our community's life. My grandfather admired that.

My grandfather was a popular person in high school. He was senior class president and married his high school sweetheart while still in school, and they had a son named Oscar. Everyone was concerned for my grandfather because of these heavy responsibilities with a new wife and child. Kansas City was pretty tough for him, and he saw it severely limiting him in reaching his goals. His wife's sister lived in Minnesota, and she suggested moving up north because it had better opportunities for African Americans and way less discrimination toward them. In 1922, at the age of 19, Cecil Newman by himself went right to his sister-in-law's home in South Minneapolis. His plan was to get a job and then get his own place to stay, then bring up his new family. He ended up getting a job at the Minneapolis Elks Club as a bellhop. He also eventually got a writing job for the local Black newspaper called *The Northwestern Bulletin-Appeal*.

The Northwestern Bulletin-Appeal was a combination of two struggling Black newspapers in St. Paul at the time, the *Western Appeal* (or *The Appeal*) and *The Northwestern Bulletin*. Roy Wilkins (future secretary of the national NAACP) was *The Appeal's* editor, and it was the official publication of the United Brotherhood of Railway Porters (Hasso 2021). So Wilkins worked with A. Philip Randolph, leader of the Brotherhood of Sleeping Car Porters on a variety of issues. In 1923, just as my grandfather got here, Wilkins went to Kansas City, Missouri, to be the editor of *The Call*. It was like my grandfather and Wilkins literally switched places.

Many Black men at that time were Pullman porters, traveling the country to all the major cities and connecting with African American communities throughout. These men were exposed to various voices of the Black community and, as porters, they distributed Black newspapers to cities on their routes. This served as the Black grapevine in our community. The porters primarily distributed five major Black newspapers: the *Baltimore Afro-American*, *The Chicago Defender*, *The New York Age*, *New York Amsterdam News*, and *The Pittsburgh Courier*. My grandfather met and worked with many porters and ended up getting a job as one. This is where he made enough money to bring his wife and son up from Kansas City. My grandfather also wrote for several of these papers as a freelance journalist.

In 1925, *The Northwestern Bulletin-Appeal* closed. This unfortunate circumstance gave Mr. Newman an opportunity to get a step closer to his dream by cofounding, with J.E. Perry, the *Twin-City Herald* newspaper in Minneapolis. However, my grandfather had greater visions of starting his own publication, which he did in 1934, the *Minneapolis Spokesman*. At that time, he decided it was hard enough to raise money for one newspaper, so if he had two, that would double his income. So he started the *St. Paul Recorder* simultaneously. The name came from our slogan: "As it was spoken, let us record." So, we got the *Spokesman* and the *Recorder* from that. Mr. Newman opened a little storefront over in South Minneapolis, then ended up moving to another building in downtown Minneapolis at 309 3rd Street South. In 1954, my grandfather bought and moved into our current location at 3744 4th Avenue South. The building used to be a warehouse that had a great big printing machine. My grandfather hired two white guys to print the paper every week for years. After Mr. Newman passed away, my grandmother, my uncle, and my mother ran the paper together; they closed the press and contracted an outside press to print our paper.

Mr. Newman did everything from management, advertising sales, writing, and distribution. But his dream was finally realized when he saw his name in print with Publisher and Editor behind it on page 2. My grandfather wrote the editorials in his newspapers in a section called the Publisher's Corner. He also wrote a weekly Black history column titled Our Past This Week.

My grandfather, as the voice of the Black community, obtained some clout. People Black and white called upon him when they were addressing various community issues. White politicians and business leaders sought his advice and council on how to best address white and Black relations. My grandfather had an activist paper in that he would publicly support businesses that were fair to Black people, and he would call out businesses that mistreated us or wouldn't hire us. He also told the stories about our community: who's doing what, who was hired somewhere, who accomplished what, and who married who.

My grandfather mentored, trained, and gave opportunities to many people in our community—for instance, Gordon Parks, the famous photographer for *Life* and *Vogue* magazines, who later went on to become a major filmmaker. Gordon started off with Mr. Newman as a photographer, writer, and circulation manager. Gordon had a column called Beauty of the Week. We think *Jet* magazine was inspired by this idea and put it in full color. Ethel Ray Nance, the Civil Rights activist and assistant to W.E.B. Du Bois, was an associate editor with Mr. Newman for the *Timely Digest*, a full-color magazine my grandfather tried to start for a couple of years. We also believe this magazine was an inspiration for John H. Johnson's *Ebony* magazine. Ethel Ray Nance also wrote in the *St. Paul Recorder* and the *Minneapolis Spokesman* newspapers. Carl Rowan, the prominent journalist, author, and government official, started his journalist career with my grandfather at the *Spokesman-Recorder* after he graduated from the University of Minnesota with a master's in journalism. Rowan became one of the first Black staff writers for *The Minneapolis Tribune* and wrote a nationally syndicated column. Era Bell Thompson—the *Ebony* managing editor and prominent author who was from Des Moines, went to school in North Dakota, and lived in St. Paul for a short time—worked for my grandfather at the *Twin-City Herald* as a typist and writer.

When I look at the patterns and the path that I went down with little to no knowledge of my grandfather's path, I see a lot of similarities. I watched and studied him. I read his biography written by L. Edmond Leipold in 1969 and his personal journal.

Passing on the Legacy

The legacy of the *Minneapolis Spokesman* and the *St. Paul Recorder* wasn't apparent to me while growing up. However, the newspapers were my life. I don't remember a time when we did not have hundreds of copies of newspapers at home, or when I was not at the MSR offices during my childhood. Whether going to visit my grandparents or mother or going to the offices to work, one could say I wasn't conscious of my legacy.

Journalism was never something I wanted to do. I was a people person so I wanted to go into a career where I could help people. My high school career goal was to become a chemical dependency counselor, which I was really intrigued by the possibility of doing. I was also a hustler at a young age. I started working when I was 14 years old at my first real summer job (outside of the paper), and I never stopped working. My youngest brother used to call me TCF (Twin Cities Federal Bank) because if my siblings needed to borrow some money, I was like, "What do you need?" I always had money because I always worked. My grandmother saw that work ethic in me. I did go to college and get trained as a chemical abuse counselor. I worked at Turning Point, which provided chemical health, housing, supporting services, and training for the African American community. It was called the Institute on Black Chemical Abuse back when I worked for them.

I always knew that I could work at the *Spokesman-Recorder*. My grandmother brought me in at the age of 8 working there every Wednesday. My main job was using the Addressograph machine to put address labels on the newspapers. Once the labels were created, there was a slot in the printer that you fed the papers through. I created label plates until I was 17, then I learned how to do billing for subscriptions and ads. As a young adult, although I had my own career, I worked as human resources at MSR and I was like a mediator between my mom, my uncle, and the staff. I began doing more management work.

With my early and consistent exposure, I had been prepared to run the paper all along. You plant a seed and then you water it in the hope it grows. So that's what my grandmother was doing. She planted the seed by bringing us in. Vicky and I were the main two, because we were old enough to understand how to do certain things. Over time, I took on more responsibilities. This was my summer job starting in junior high. After listening to my inner calling and accepting my legacy, I started looking at the newspaper differently. I saw that MSR helped thousands of people. I realized I had the opportunity to really help in a much bigger way.

Prior to my grandmother passing, she was very active in many different clubs. She would always tell her friends and club members that she was thinking about handing the paper over to me. They often would come and tell me that my grandmother talked about me and had a lot of pride in me, because she raised me up at the MSR and knew I could take the paper over and run it successfully one day.

In 2000, the paper was under threat of being sold outside the family. If I had not stepped in, it would likely be owned by somebody else right now. My mother and uncle weren't the happiest when my grandmother gave me the reins. However, the paper was in big trouble and needed a family member leading it who had visions similar to that of my grandfather. I reorganized my family and the staff and got the paper back to its mission. During the transition we did not lose any subscribers; however, we did not pick up any significant readership either.

The younger generation does not use newspapers as we did. Social media is their primary source of information. We're evolving, and we're trying to figure out how to embrace more young readers. There are still some students who will pick up a newspaper and read a book. They still want to read news, even though they read it on the internet. Our young adults still want community news as well. So we still have a niche that we are targeting, and we have news and information for the students who are looking for news and information. We want to be sure to embrace them. We also have the blessing of having younger staff members. We are still all over young African American sports in the metro area through our sports writers who have been here for decades. Sports have always been a big deal in our community, and we are able to get a lot of our youth in our newspaper and on our website.

Our subscription base is still here because of the grandmothers who are still with us and still pick up our newspaper. We still have some of the grandkids, now in their 40s and 50s, who get the paper because they remember their grandmothers getting it and how important it was to them. We currently have a readership of 10,000 people, and so we print 10,000 papers each week. Our online newspaper is popular too, and we do reach the younger reader. We were challenged by the community distribution of the paper because trying to be everywhere is very costly. You need someone to deliver them each week. Somebody must pick the old ones up. We had to pay for that service. The old paper carrier concept is gone. Since taking over the *Spokesman-Recorder*, I've been trying to organize our community distribution a little differently now. We are stronger now than we were before.

George Floyd—The Impact

Unfortunately, the world knows George Floyd's name now and the injustice that was perpetrated. The tragedy is known worldwide. Everybody knows about it. The humanity of Black people was recognized among more white people in this country and by people around the world. Like in the 1950s and 1960s, mainstream media—newspapers, magazines, television—showed the world the brutality of white people toward the Black citizens of this country, and some white people took note and some change occurred. It appears that some people forgot that justice is a process, because in 2020, George Floyd, an unarmed Black man, was murdered not just by Derek Chauvin, a white police officer, but by a criminal justice system that has been oppressing African Americans since the founding of this country. America was reminded of their inhumanity and acts of injustice toward Black people. Once again, America is trying to figure out what to do with us. Mainstream media attempted to do news coverage that included other perspectives beside white Americans and be politically correct. This has been a systemic issue for years with mainstream media, and they still aren't writing about issues that affect Black lives in any significant way.

The aftermath of George Floyd in 2020 was very difficult for me and the paper. I would pull up to our building on 4th Avenue, twelve blocks from where George Floyd was murdered, and it was boarded up due to the rebellion. My emotions were so high. I was sad and felt defeated. I was like, If the building is boarded up, then the paper is boarded up too. I was like, We're done. We're closed for good! That's the feeling that came over me. I sat in my car in front of our building, and I just broke down in tears. This incident, the aftermath, and the impact on our community was emotionally too much. It was the hardest thing to pull up in front of our building, after all these years, and it was boarded up. It was devastating.

I remember thinking that the Black Press is more important now than ever. MSR was at ground zero of the George Floyd incident, and many news and media outlets came to us looking for the story. Although this was flattering and we got noticed more, it did not translate into money or support for our business as it should have. Even mainstream media knocked on our door, something that never really happened before. This showed me their limitations and/or willingness to connect with our community. Who in mainstream media is going to continue to advocate for our needs, care about our interests, and tell our hidden stories? Black Minnesotans don't go to the *Star Tribune* or Channel 11, 5, 9, or 4 for advocacy or for the truth about the Black community's narratives and perspectives, unless you see Black people in a protest that they're covering. The spirit of my ancestors told me that I was going to wake up, stand up, and thrive. And that's what I did.

The mainstream media are really puppets on a string. If you look at their funding sources, governance boards, and policies, then you can see the limitations of their actions and their will to be truly inclusive. Although we may see Black faces in the mainstream in the form of Black journalists, there is a white person behind them that's writing, telling, and approving their story. The white people still have the rights to the story and still edit the content. Most Black journalists in those organizations are not able to control their content or what they produce.

Businesses, organizations, and government entities made many published public statements about supporting the Black community after the George Floyd incident and supposedly understood that their past lack of support for justice and community development is what led to this eruption in our community again. Four years later, these same businesses, organizations, and government entities have forgotten that we have those statements still and they haven't fulfilled their public promises. It's like in the 1960s and 1970s after the rebellions following the assassination of Dr. Martin Luther King Jr. Money was given for a few years and programs started, after which many of these entities thought they were done with supporting the community and implementing measures of justice. The mainstream media published essentially that things were good while ignoring the continued pain and injustice happening in the Black community. The Black Press had the stick-to-it power. In 2024, once again like most tragedies, when the smoke clears, we can go back to business as usual. That's where the *Spokesman-Recorder* and other Black media come in. We aren't letting up. We continue to hold the mainstream media and our country accountable through our stories and truth telling.

Starting diversity, equity, and inclusion, or DEI, programs may be an initial step for many of these businesses, but it should not be the last step. My grandfather Cecil Newman spent his years at the paper ensuring businesses allowed Black people into their establishment and then made sure they hired us. Many white businesses, concerned about their existence, hired Black faces simply as an economic decision, because they would be boycotted or given bad press if they did not. The hires were not about the Black community for the most part. Systemic quality change was not in the cards. Ultimately, it came down to their profit line. Community investment and justice doesn't do that; in fact, it was often an exploitative relationship with our community that some of these businesses had.

Back in my grandfather's time, our community and the broader community knew the power of the pen and what a story could do. Today, many in the younger generation of the Black community don't realize the power of the pen. As we can see with the banning of books and the banning of Black history in several states, there is a continued attempt to keep the masses ignorant. The schools still aren't doing a great job even teaching the basics such as reading, so we can't read or we don't read. There's an old saying that states, "The best way to keep a secret from a Black person is to put it in a book." It appears the young Black generation under 40 has forsaken books and newspapers and has chosen social media for excerpts of news and stories.

Legacy: Past and Present

I think being a family-owned business means that people feel we're a part of the community. The paper hasn't sold out or been bought by a bigger conglomerate. They feel we still represent a community that we're a part of tangibly. I think it's important for readers in the community to know that we're still family-owned and run. Our community trusts that we will get it and understand what's going on with them. We understand the community's needs, hurts, and hopes. We come from a diverse Black community with different demographic areas, and we have different views and, in some cases, even different values. When you have a homegrown family newspaper that has a family tradition and reflects the mainstream values of the community, I think that means a lot to a community.

Like my grandfather did, I want the paper to educate, inform, and inspire. We have a tradition and responsibility to support Black businesses. We highlight businesses in our paper. We advertise for businesses. We host gatherings for businesses to network and for community members to meet with them. Some businesses carry our paper. We share information that benefits our businesses. The *St. Paul Recorder* was on the front line advocating against the interstate freeway in the 1950s going through the heart of the St. Paul Black community. The *Recorder* documented the impact on the housing and displacement of people from the Rondo neighborhood and of the Black businesses and organizations that would possibly be destroyed and never return. Today, in 2024, we are on the front line of sharing information on how we are still trying to recover and heal and seek justice for the past harm to our community. However, today we do it as one newspaper, the *Minnesota Spokesman-Recorder*. Since its inception in the 1930s the newspaper has been a statewide and regional publication with correspondents in places like Duluth; Rochester; Sioux Falls, South Dakota; and Mason City, Iowa. Still, my grandmother, before she transitioned the newspaper, had the discussion with the family about the paper serving more than Minneapolis and St. Paul. Today, there are over 400,000 Black people or people of African Heritage living in Minnesota, primarily in the seven-county metro area, but Black people live in over 60 percent of the 850-plus cities in Minnesota. We serve them too. As MSR approaches a new millennium, we are expanding in concert with our constituents to serve the changing demographics of the African globe and community. Our goal is to unite, serve, and represent that constituency.

The stories we tell, I want them to be able to reach you as an individual reader. I want you to see yourself in the stories because now it means something to you. So that's why our storytelling is important, so that people can see themselves. We don't do a lot of negative news unless it's against us, not about us. The other media outlets handle that negative aspect about us very well. I think that African Americans, and people in general, need to understand the importance of why MSR needs to exist. For example, I don't know how to tell that little boy, who walks down the street with his pants hanging down and who doesn't even know what this building is that he just walked past, that we at MSR need to matter to him. Because one day, when he needs somebody to tell his story, he's going to walk through this door. Because he can't go downtown to the *Star Tribune* or Channel 11 and get his story told. MSR needs to do a better job of educating and sharing what our role is in the community, our past and current impact, and why the community needs to support this institution. It really is about that consciousness. We have seen what happens to our businesses and organizations when we take them for granted. They disappear and we ask, "What happened?"

My grandfather, when he started this newspaper, opened so many doors for Black people in this city. Without him, they wouldn't have had the opportunities afforded to them to do what they did, to be who they were. Consequently, they had respect for him as a Black man. He was not a loud, boisterous bullhorn. He was a nice, mild-tempered, smart man. He had the respect of the people at City Hall and at the Capitol. He was political too. I, on the other hand, am not a politician. He was opinionated and wrote his opinions weekly in the newspaper. I don't. I allow the facts and information from the stories we share with you to persuade you. If we give you enough information, you can make an informed decision about what's going on and what you think you should do about it. My grandfather used the strength of his paper to hold the various powers that be accountable, whether they were businesses, corporations, or the government. He wouldn't let up until he saw change. He would write; he used his voice for change. I use storytelling for change. He was more of an activist. I'm more of an educator and community connector. However, I do need to be more like my grandfather. In the aftermath of George Floyd's murder, a lot of corporations publicly stated they would be supporting our businesses and investing in our community. They have not come through as they had promised, which is wrong. MSR and I will be calling upon these institutions and corporations to keep their word and invest. We may have to hold some of these so-called "allies" accountable in ink, like my grandfather did in the past.

How do you support Black newspapers in today's world? First, we must understand the importance of Black media. If we are a Black/African American community, then we need operational unity and support. The Hmong and Somali communities in Minnesota are great examples of this regarding the practice of supporting businesses within their communities. Below are some practices that can help support Black newspapers and media:

1. Start by getting a yearly subscription to one or more Black newspapers. Find out how many of your family members have subscriptions. How many people in your organization, club, and/or church have subscriptions? If you had a subscription to a Black paper that has lapsed, when do you plan to renew it? Do you see our papers in our schools and colleges? Educational institutions and libraries must subscribe too. As parents and taxpayers, we need to demand that our voice be in those places.

2. Sign up online for online Black papers at no cost.

3. Advertise businesses and organizations in Black papers.

4. Support the businesses and organizations that advertise in Black papers.

5. Place your legal notices and job announcements in Black papers.

6. Share new tips and stories with Black papers.

7. Become a freelance writer for Black papers.

8. Write a Letter to the Editor about some issue to be published in a Black paper.
9. Support and come to events and programs sponsored by Black papers.

References:

Hasso, Jennifer. 2021. "Pullman Porters." Jim Crow Museum. https://jimcrowmuseum.ferris.edu/question/2021/august.htm.

Leipold, L. Edmond. 1969. *Cecil E. Newman: Newspaper Publisher*. Minneapolis, MN: T.S. Denison.

St. Paul Recorder:

August 11, 1939: Photograph by Gordon Parks, staff photographer, of Miss Alice Short. Page 1.

December 10, 1943: "Gordon Parks, War Correspondent, Visits at Home." Page 1.

October 24, 1947: Publisher's Corner. Page. 4.

August 27, 1948: Geri Hoffner. "Editor Backs Up All Minorities." *Minneapolis Tribune*. Reprint by *St. Paul Recorder*. Page 6.

March 21, 1952: "Editor First Minnesota Negro Listed in Who's Who In America." Page 4.

August 24, 1956: Publisher's Corner. Page 2.

April 11, 1963: Our Past This Week: "Clip for Negro History Scrapbook." Page 2.

Tracey L. Williams-Dillard

Tracey Lynn Williams-Dillard has always been driven by her dedication to her multigenerational family and their family business. As CEO of the *Minnesota Spokesman-Recorder*, Tracey is responsible for day-to-day operations and strategic direction of the newspaper. Her vision, passion, and commitment have been instrumental in carrying the newspaper into the future, more than nine decades after its founding by her grandfather, the late Cecil E. Newman, in 1934.

Tracey's journey with the paper began at the age of 8, when she learned how to operate the Addressograph machine. Over the years, she has held various roles within the organization, including receptionist, billing, and advertising sales representative.

In 2001, Tracey became president of the 89-year-old newspaper, and in 2006, she assumed the role of owner and CEO. She is on the MSR board of directors and is president of the *Spokesman-Recorder* Nonprofit.

In 2006, Tracey founded Sister Spokesman, a group that provides women of color with monthly networking and learning opportunities. The group continues to thrive, with monthly attendance averaging 75 to 100 participants. One of Tracey's proudest achievements is the launch, in 1995, of the *Spokesman-Recorder*'s annual Graduation Celebration: A Family Affair. This event celebrates the educational milestones of African and African American graduating seniors and their families, emphasizing the importance of education to the future of Black Americans

11

How Publisher Cecil Newman Made His Mark on the Minnesota Newspaper Industry

Daniel Pierce Bergin

Cecil Newman was a pioneering newspaper publisher and influential leader in Minnesota. His newspapers, the *Minneapolis Spokesman* and the *St. Paul Recorder*, provided news and information to readers while advancing Civil Rights, fair employment, political engagement, and Black pride.

Cecil Earl Newman was born in Kansas City, Missouri, in 1903. He transcended the limits of segregated education and became the editor of his school paper. As a teen, he delivered African American newspapers as he hoped for a future in the publishing business.

In the early 1920s, Newman headed north to distance himself from the reach of Southern racism and settled in Minneapolis. Work as a porter in the railroad industry offered him a decent wage. When he applied for work with mainstream newspapers in the Twin Cities, however, he was refused on the basis of race, so he began working with the long-standing Black paper *The Northwestern Bulletin-Appeal*. He also wrote as a freelance reporter or "stringer" for notable Black newspapers, including *The Chicago Defender*. In 1927, Newman and J.E. Perry cofounded the *Twin-City Herald* paper in Minneapolis, with Newman serving as editor and Perry as publisher.

After seven years at the *Herald*, Newman resolved to become the publisher of his own publications, and the summer of 1934 saw the first edition of the *Minneapolis Spokesman* roll off the presses. Its twin, the *St. Paul Recorder*, followed. In both papers, Newman pledged to "speak out fearlessly and unceasingly against injustices, discriminations, and all imposed inequities."

Like other Black papers of the era, the *Spokesman* and the *Recorder* were filled with local and national news, entertainment, social and church affairs, and other content of interest to African Americans. The early version included a gossip column called Inquisitive Sal, comics and cartoons drawn by Black artists, sports coverage, and classified ads aimed at African Americans.

Newman also saw speaking to white readers—and white advertisers—as important to furthering equity and inclusion. The *Spokesman* and the *Recorder* became training grounds for Black leaders and literary luminaries like Era Bell Thompson, Gordon Parks, and Carl Rowan.

Newman's pledge to utilize the printing press as a clarion for Civil Rights led to a confrontation with the local beer industry. The 1933 repeal of Prohibition had led to growth for Minnesota's brewers, and the *Spokesman* charged that despite the expansion of jobs, these breweries refused to employ a single African American. Newman called for a boycott of local breweries, including Hamm's and Gluek's, in the spring of 1935. The effective campaign featured opinion pieces from Newman and front-page editorial cartoons ridiculing the brewers.

During World War II, Newman successfully fought for African American access to jobs at local munitions plants, including the Twin Cities Army Ammunition Plant. Two decades later he would push the owner of the newly arrived Minnesota Twins to desegregate spring training lodgings.

Newman's close connection with Minneapolis Mayor Hubert Humphrey began a decades-long alliance with the statesman. When Humphrey and Lyndon Johnson won the White House in 1964, there was an opportunity for Newman to join his old friend on the national stage, according to Newman's granddaughter Tracey Williams-Dillard. However, he demurred, choosing to stay in South Minneapolis and continue his journalistic and civic leadership in Minnesota, where he gained membership to several fraternal, civic, Civil Rights, and business leadership organizations.

Newman's network wasn't limited to the Democratic-Farmer-Labor Party (DFL). In his lifetime, he claimed a connection to every Minnesota governor since the 1920s. He was also close to moderate, business-minded

Republicans like Wheelock Whitney Jr., to the chagrin of some progressives in the Black community. In the late 1960s, a rock was thrown through the window of the *Spokesman* building, allegedly by Black radicals who saw Newman as out of touch (according to reports of the incident).

With the rise of new and more radical leadership in the Civil Rights movement, and now in his later years, Newman receded into the background of civic and Civil Rights activity. He died in February of 1976. Activist, youth worker, and community leader Spike Moss eulogized the late publisher with the simple, powerful affirmation: "Cecil Soldiered."

Following the leadership of Newman's widow, Launa Newman, Newman's granddaughter Tracey Williams-Dillard took the helm of the *Minnesota Spokesman-Recorder*, and it is among a dwindling number of historic Black newspapers that have survived into the 2020s. With his decades of journalism, his legacy as one of Minnesota's great civic and Civil Rights leaders, Cecil Newman could be called, like his paper, Spokesman.

Resources

Ampers. 2015. "Cecil E. Newman: A Strong Black Leader." *MinneHistory*. KFAI. http://ampers.org/mn-art-culture-history/cecil-e-newman-a-strong-black-leader.

"Cecil Newman." 1972. People Worth Hearing About. Minnesota School of the Air, WLB/KUOM, University of Minnesota Libraries Archive, April 6, 1972. www.archives.lib.umn.edu/repositories/14/archival_objects/1023282.

Coleman, Milton. 1976. "Cecil Newman: A Spirit of Patient Civility." *Minneapolis Star*, February 11, 1976.

Glanton, Wayne. 2015. Interview with the author.

Henehan, Brendan. 2002. "Minnesota Black Newspaper Index." Unpublished manuscript, last modified 2002. Minnesota Historical Society.

http://www.mnhs.org/duluthlynchings/resources/blacknewspaperindex.pdf.

Leipold, L. Edmond. 1969. *Cecil E. Newman: Newspaper Publisher*. Minneapolis, MN: T.S. Denison.

Mikus, Matt. 2021. "'Super Cool': Minnesota's Oldest Black-owned Newspaper Puts Its Archive Online." MPR News, May 30, 2021. https://www.mprnews.org/story/2021/05/30/minnesotas-oldest-blackowned-newspaper-puts-its-archive-online.

Minneapolis Spokesman. 1934–2000. Minnesota Digital Newspaper Hub, Minnesota Historical Society. https://newspapers.mnhs.org/jsp/browse.jsp?collection_filter=6ff34a0f-54f7-4bc3-861a-d07acb7dba65.

Minneapolis Star. 1960. "Why Was It Necessary to Handcuff Kline?" August 13, 1960.

Minneapolis Star. 1963. "Twins Work to End Bias at Training Site." January 31, 1963.

Minneapolis Star. 1964. "Rocks Hit Window of Newspaper." August 31, 1964.

MSR News Online. 2015. "MSR Building Now a Historic Minnesota Landmark." November 23, 2015. https://spokesman-recorder.com/2015/11/23/msr-building-now-historic-minnesota-landmark.

Nathanson, Iric. "Spokesman for the Community: Cecil Newman and His Legacy of African American Journalism." *Hennepin History* 69, no. 3 (Fall 2010): 4–21. Hennepin County Library Digital Collections. https://digitalcollections.hclib.org/digital/collection/p17208coll13/id/2354.

New York Times. 1976. "Cecil E. Newman, Headed Minneapolis Black Weekly." February 8, 1976. https://www.nytimes.com/1976/02/08/archives/cecil-e-newman-headed-minneapolis-black-weekly.html.

St. Paul Recorder. 1934–2000. Minnesota Digital Newspaper Hub, Minnesota Historical Society. https://newspapers.mnhs.org/jsp/browse.jsp?collection_filter=578670e0-fcaf-4562-a166-28850a1922dd.

Williams-Dillard, Tracey. 2015. Interview with the author.

12

Reclaiming My Historical Imagination

Lissa Jones-Lofgren

One day it was just gone. Lost. Vanished. Disappeared.

The kind of gone that makes you doubt whether you actually had it in the first place.

I host a podcast, called *Black Market Reads,* with the mission to amplify the voices of Black authors and to honor their contributions to the literary canon. To prepare for my interview of Patricia Smith, I'd just finished reading her book of poems *Incendiary Art:*

> Emmett Till: Choose Your Own Adventure
>
> Mamie Till had hoped to take her son, Emmett, on a vacation to visit relatives in Nebraska. Instead, he begged her to let him visit his cousins in Mississippi[1].

The Choose Your Own Adventure series is a collection of children's game books where each story is narrated from a second-person perspective, putting the reader directly in the role of the protagonist. As the stories unfold, the reader makes key decisions that influence the character's actions and ultimately shape the outcome of the plot. Smith's poems offer searing observations, wise critiques on the realities of Black life, and, most importantly, the agency to choose how her poems end.

At the time of my realization, I was fully immersed in serving my community. I was creating *Urban Agenda,* a weekly public affairs show on KMOJ Radio[2], and hosting the *Black Market Reads* podcast[3]. As the executive director of African American Family Services, I was dedicated to helping individuals heal by uplifting and teaching Black history, culture, and healing traditions. I spoke nationally on issues impacting Black life and culture, striving to build a bridge between historical events and present-day realities for Black Americans, shaped by my own experiences. My life was devoted to service, and it had never crossed my mind to consider what might have been if Emmett Till had "never gone South in the first damn place":

> Mamie Till insisted on an open casket so that the world could see her son's mutilated body. More than 50,000 people filed past during his funeral. Many screamed or fainted.
>
> Turn to page 27 if Emmett's casket was closed instead[4].

How did it happen? Where did it go? When did I lose it? Did someone take it? The "it" was my historical imagination—and, with it, the agency that accompanies it. Early in my scholarship, my mentor Mahmoud El-Kati[5] taught us that the loss of historical imagination is a consequence of white supremacy. Despite learning and teaching about the myths of "race" and the realities of racism[6], I found myself so fixated on the "facts" that I lost the ability to envision something beyond the tragedies that history can often present. I had unwittingly surrendered the power to choose my own narrative and imagine a different future.

It is hard, maybe impossible, to convey how sobering the moment felt. Am I an imposter? Have I been robbing my listeners of their historical imagination too? Did I *willingly* give up my agency to dream of different outcomes? When did I last choose my own adventure? Whose stories was I telling?

The murder of 14-year-old Emmett Till in 1955 shocked the nation, drawing attention to the pervasive racial violence and injustice in Mississippi. During a visit to his relatives, Till went to the Bryant store with his cousins, where he allegedly whistled at Carolyn Bryant. This incident led to his kidnapping and brutal murder by Carolyn's husband, Roy Bryant, and her brother-in-law, J.W. Milam. They dumped Till's mutilated body in the Tallahatchie River.

Choose Your Own Adventure

Turn to page 48 if Emmett Till's body is never found[7].

In the Bridges Transition Model[8], every transition begins with an ending, and something shifts. The day I came to the recognition of my loss of imagination was the day something shifted, the day I was thrown into transition, without my permission.

The second phase in the Bridges Transition Model is the neutral zone: "The essence of life takes place in the neutral zone phase of transition. It is in that interim spaciousness that all possibilities, creativity and innovative ideas can come to life and flourish."[9] I wish I could say the transition process is linear, that it follows a timeline, that it is all joy, that grief is not present . . . but I can tell you that the neutral zone led me to the new beginnings in the Bridges' thinking!

My time in the neutral zone was likely shorter than I remember and longer than I think; memory can play tricks on you. What I do remember is when I got the clarity, saw the way back, I felt joy again! I committed to the revolutionary act of *re-remembering*, the act of remembering again. Lucille Clifton helped me understand that remembering my memories is a revolutionary act!

why people be mad at me sometimes

they ask me to remember
but they want me to remember
their memories
and i keep on remembering
mine.
—Lucille Clifton[10]

Current Ruminations +

Who could "we" be?

.if no kidnap

..if no stolen labor or land

...if no "race"

....if human first and only

.....if relationships over transactions

......if no harm done so no reparations needed

.......if the health of the children was our measure of quality of life

.... if we choose our own adventure!

End Notes

1. Patricia Smith, *Incendiary Art*, 2017.

2. KMOJ Radio is a Black-centered cultural institution, one of precious few in Minnesota, est. 1976.

3. *Black Market Reads* is a podcast of the Givens Foundation for African American Literature.

4. Patricia Smith, *Incendiary Art*, 2017.

5. Mahmoud El-Kati, chair emeritus of American History, Macalester College.

6. Mahmoud El-Kati, *The Myth of Race/The Reality of Racism*, 1993.

7. Patricia Smith, *Incendiary Art*, 2017.

8. Developed by William Bridges, the Bridges Transition Model has been used by leaders and management consultants for more than thirty years.

9. Susan Bridges, William Bridges Associates.

10. A prolific and widely respected poet, Lucille Clifton's work emphasizes endurance and strength through adversity, focusing particularly on African American experience and family life.

References

Bridges, Susan. 2024. Bridges Transition Model. https://wmbridges.com/about/what-is-transition/.

Bridges, William. 2024. Bridges Transition Model. https://wmbridges.com/about/what-is-transition/.

Clifton, Lucille. 2021. "why people be mad at me sometimes." SALT Project. https://www.saltproject.org/progressive-christian-blog/2021/5/25/why-some-people-be-mad-at-me-sometimes-by-lucille-clifton.

El-Kati, Mahmoud. 1993. *The Myth of Race/The Reality of Racism*. St. Paul, MN: Stairstep Foundation.

Smith, Patricia. 2017. *Incendiary Art*: *Poems*. Evanston, IL: TriQuarterly Books/Northwestern University Press.

Lissa Jones-Lofgren

Lissa Jones-Lofgren is a distinguished executive leader with extensive experience driving organizational change and fostering inclusive cultures. As a seasoned Fractional CEO and Organizational Behaviorist, Lissa specializes in guiding organizations through complex transformations, aligning missions with strategic goals, and cultivating environments where diversity, equity, and inclusion are not just ideals but practiced values.

With a proven track record as an executive director and interim leader, Lissa has successfully led teams through periods of significant change, always with a focus on operational excellence and cultural integrity. Her expertise in governance, strategic planning, and stakeholder engagement has made her a trusted advisor and coach to leaders and boards committed to achieving meaningful and sustainable impact.

Lissa is also a sought-after speaker and facilitator, known for her ability to challenge organizations to move beyond superficial inclusion measures to embrace true diversity and equity. She spent fifteen years as the host and content creator of *Urban Agenda* on KMOJ Radio, where she remained deeply connected to the community she represents. Currently, she hosts the acclaimed podcast *Black Market Reads* for the Givens Foundation for African American Literature, amplifying the voices of Black authors and exploring the rich tapestry of African American literature.

In addition to her executive roles, Lissa served as the Chair of the University of Minnesota Friends of the Libraries, reflecting her commitment to literacy, cultural equity, and community engagement. A lifelong Minnesotan, Lissa's leadership is deeply rooted in her understanding of the communities she serves and her unwavering dedication to advancing social justice.

13

Hear the Children

Donnie Nicole Belcher

We have all heard the motto "Children are to be seen and not to be heard." This sentiment has silenced an entire segment of our community. Young people are spoken *at*, spoken *for*, and spoken *about*. The first "platform" all young people should have access to is the ears of their parents and the hearts of their families, long before they ever enter a classroom, months before they can repeat and regurgitate their ABCs, light-years before they ever sign up for social media.

One of the most meaningful gifts I ever received as a child was a diary. This gift was important to me because it was an indirect way to tell me that my thoughts, my feelings, and my voice mattered. While I grew up in an extended family that very much subscribed to the "Children are to be seen and not heard" philosophy, my grandmother and mother regularly created space for me, an only child, to share my opinions and thoughts about all sorts of things. My earliest memories of media-making came from growing up in the African Methodist Episcopal, Zion and African Methodist Episcopal traditions. Every Sunday, a young person who was "good at reading" would be assigned the task of reading the announcements. Another young person was responsible for reading the scriptures and participating in other call and response activities. This experience taught me the difference between how my voice sounded in my diary versus how it sounded—amplified, loud, commanding—in the microphone. I can remember my unfiltered voice in my diary, which would sometimes be intercepted by my mother ("Who IS this boy? Why are you cursing? Where did you learn about this?"), versus my polished voice at the lectern behind the altar: sanctified, dignified, distinguished. I am so grateful for the adults in my life who understood the importance of connecting me to my voice as a young person. These experiences laid the foundation of literacy for me.

Once I got to high school, THE North Community High School, in North Minneapolis, I had an opportunity to focus on the arts. I chose "writing as performance" as my area of focus and as a result I gained four years of being submerged in writing, literacy, and the arts. Every semester my peers and I would put on interdisciplinary performances written by and starring ourselves. This experience gave us the opportunity not only to develop as artists but to learn about production from our teachers and other mentors who worked in the field. Through the Minneapolis Urban League, I was offered an internship at *Insight News*. My direct supervisor was Batala McFarlane, now the publisher of *Insight News*. That summer internship blossomed into a four-year internship. It was at *Insight* that my English classes came to life, as I had to edit my own and other people's writing. The team created a "Youth" section where other young people could write and be featured. This was the first time I truly felt adults wanted to *hear* from young people. My experience at *Insight* also led to me becoming the 81st editor in chief of the *Polaris*, our high school newspaper. Hands-on and immersive experiences, no matter what path young people decide to take, are key to helping them find careers that align with their passions and strengths.

Youth media organizations, in all mediums, are important because they provide an opportunity to validate and affirm youth voices. School newspapers, radio stations, and, more recently, digital publications, YouTube channels, and podcasts give youth access to platforms that elevate their voices and allow them to wrestle and interact with the world. I can still remember sitting in Mrs. Brown's journalism classroom and learning about the six journalistic questions: "Who?" "What?" "When?" "Where?" "Why?" and "How?" Those basic questions taught me how to sift through text, how to frame stories, and how to prioritize information sharing and processing. In households where youth are seen and not heard, the art of the conversation and the art of storytelling is lost. In a country where it was once illegal for us to read and write, it was the oral tradition that kept us alive. The oral tradition allowed certain aspects of our culture to remain, and that links us to each other whether we find ourselves east or west of the Mississippi River or north or south of the Mason Dixon.

Social media is attractive to our young people because the barrier of entry is low. People now have the opportunity to elevate the voices and stories they care about simply by pausing their scrolling or by taking a few seconds to "like" or "save" content. Those with the highest engagement are rewarded with access to a higher volume of people. Attention literally pays. There is an old saying, "What you seek, you will find," and you can find anything on the internet, and you can find anything on social media. Teaching media literacy is more important now than it has ever been and not just to young people but to all ages. During the 2016 election between Donald Trump and Hillary Clinton, I can remember asking some of my elders where they'd heard something and they'd quickly and confidently say, "I saw it on Facebook." Our legacy institutions must learn to grasp and utilize the space of social media because it has the potential to build intergenerational relationships and modes of storytelling that marry the wisdom of the past with the future our youth are ushering in.

After leaving North High, I went on to teach high school English for fourteen years. One of the most meaningful skills I taught my students was how to conduct research. We would take deep dives into reputable or reliable versus disreputable or unreliable sources. We learned about the difference between .com and .edu and .gov. We learned that anyone could update or manipulate Wikipedia sites. Students were expected to understand the differences between scholarly articles and opinion or op-eds. Their performance assessment included writing their four-page essays with a proper thesis and either a standard or annotated bibliography. They would groan about the formality of it all. I can hear them now: "Ms . . . do we HAVE to? WHY does this matter?" I'd share with them how we had to go to a physical library when I was younger and how we had to learn how to find books physically using the Dewey Decimal system. They'd look at me like I was an alien. "Mountain Dew . . . what?" Being able to pose a question and answer a question as well as create and test a hypothesis were some of the most valuable life skills my students would ever learn. I knew this was the case, not because I wanted it to be so, but because the world is unforgiving, and ignorance is expensive. I cared deeply about my students being able to be literate—in every sense of the word.

People have been talking about the death of print media for at least the last twenty-five years. I believe that conversation parallels the death of civic education, the mass exodus of Black educators and administrators from public education, and the decline in accessible youth art- and media-focused education and programming. Our young people are being portrayed by the media as violent, apathetic, and aggressive. There are real consequences for these perceptions that are perpetuated by the media. Where are the on-ramps for youth from low-income communities to learn to PRODUCE media? When it comes to STEM programs in schools, the "A" or the "art" is often missing, as is the technological education to create media. When you enter radio stations, television studios, and newspaper offices, there is often a lack of representation behind the mic, behind the lens, and behind the press. For those of us who have been afforded the opportunity to access and, in some cases, create these platforms, we are doing ourselves a disservice if we are not also training up and finding the young people who will join and ultimately replace us. At one point it was commendable to be the exception; today it should be considered disgraceful and counterproductive to the legacies we have inherited.

Our young people are being seen and often, through no fault of their own, not in the best light. For many of our young people, they have had limited exposure to multiple pathways. You can't be what you can't see. From a young age, they have been told who and what they could and would be. During my freshman year of high school, I can remember an adult telling us, "Look to your left, look to your right . . . half of you will not graduate." It was such a dire outlook, and I can bet that many of my peers took that message to heart. That sentiment makes my skin crawl, and the fact that I still remember it is telling. That was not an affirming message. There is a place for tough love, but we need more spaces where we love tough. We need more spaces where young people are taught they can indeed do or become anything they put their minds to, and we need to give more microphones, more cameras, and more pens to young people so they can share their hopes, dreams, fears, and plans for their future, which is ultimately our shared future. I am grateful I had a family and a community who not only cared about what I had to say and what I thought but who created a space for me to share those words and thoughts. Without affirmation there is no liberation. Who are the young people in our lives and in what ways can we affirm, create space for, and elevate their voices?

Donnie's Nicole Belcher

Donnie Nicole Belcher is a lifelong educator who operates at the intersection of culture, change, and community. She was named one of *Ebony* magazine's Ebony Power 100 Honorees in 2016. After spending twelve years in the Chicago Public School system teaching literature and writing to students in grades 9–12, Donnie cofounded Art of Culture Inc., a nonprofit that cultivates youth's creative potential through arts and professional development. Donnie returned home to Minnesota in 2019 and launched Work with Donnie, a consulting firm that provides diversity, equity, and inclusion and communications services. Notable clients include the University of Minnesota and Virgin Hotels North America. She has received the Courage Award from New York University's Hip-Hop Education Center, the Deloris Jordan Award for Excellence in Community, and an Echoing Green Fellowship. Donnie currently serves as the executive director of communications and engagement for Minneapolis Public Schools and is the proud mother to Amelia Rena. For more information about Donnie, visit www.WorkWithDonnie.com.

14

A Case Study: Frederick Douglass—Literacy and Creating a Voice for His People

Al McFarlane

The value of reading and literacy is illuminated in the 1845 autobiography *Narrative of the Life of Frederick Douglass, an American Slave*. His passion for reading and writing brings tears to my eyes. Chapter VII covers Douglass learning to read and write. Here is a brief summary:

Frederick Douglass was enslaved to the Aulds. His primary job as a child was to work in the house. While working in the house, Mrs. Auld taught Douglass how to read and write. There were laws against teaching so-called "slaves" to read. Mr. Auld found out about Mrs. Auld's tutoring sessions with Douglass and put an end to them. However, the spark of learning had already been lit. Douglass would continue his learning in the broader community by giving food to poor white boys for reading lessons.

Douglass encountered a book called *The Columbian Orator,* a collection of political essays, poems, and dialogues collected and written by Caleb Bingham and published in 1797, which contains speeches by George Washington, Benjamin Franklin, and some imagined speeches by historical figures such as Socrates and Cato. This book often was used in schools from 1790 to 1820 to teach pupils reading and speaking. One of the essays expounds a philosophical dialogue between a master and a slave. In the dialogue, the master lays out the argument for slavery, and the slave refutes each point, eventually convincing the master to release him. The book also contains a reprint of a speech arguing for the emancipation of Irish Catholics and for human rights generally. Douglass bought this book for 50 cents at the age of 12 and cited it as his inspiration and training text that he used to become the great orator, thinker, and writer he eventually became.

During this period, Douglass eagerly listened to anyone discussing slavery. He learned what an "abolitionist" was and what "antislavery" meant. Douglass secretly read newspapers, opening up his understanding of the enormous enterprise of slavery and the millions of Africans enslaved and controlled by white slave masters. Douglass had known intuitively that slavery was evil but did not know how it worked. His master's pronouncement that education ruins slaves was telling to Douglass. He suddenly understood that white owners gain and keep power over slaves by depriving them of education. Douglass realized that, in addition to physically escaping enslavement, he must become educated to become free. The idea that education is the means to freedom is a major theme in the narrative and, at 12 years old, Douglass became resolute to become free.

Douglass eventually learned to write and became one of the most famous activists, orators, authors, and journalists of the nineteenth century.

And what if Douglass never did read or write?

Then we would not have had access to his four major newspapers:

The North Star (Rochester, New York), 1847–1851
Douglass founded and edited his first antislavery newspaper, *The North Star*, beginning on December 3, 1847. The title referred to the bright star Polaris that helped guide those escaping slavery to the North, and the newspaper was intended to "promote the moral and intellectual improvement of the colored people."

Frederick Douglass' Paper (Rochester, New York), 1851–1860
In June 1851, *The North Star* merged with the *Liberty Party Paper* (Syracuse, New York), under the title *Frederick Douglass' Paper*. Published with the volume and issue numbering continuing from *The North Star*, Douglass remained editor.

Douglass' Monthly (Rochester, New York), 1859–1863
Beginning as a supplement to the *Frederick Douglass' Paper*, the *Douglass' Monthly* became an independent publication the following year and was distributed until 1863.

New National Era (Washington, D.C.), 1870–1874
His final newspaper venture began in September 1870 when Douglass became editor in chief and part owner of the *New National Era* in Washington, D.C. He was a corresponding editor based out of Rochester, New York.

We would perhaps not know the righteous encouragement Frederick Douglass delivered on August 3, 1857, in his "West India Emancipation" speech at Canandaigua, New York:

> Those who profess to favor freedom and yet depreciate agitation, are people who want crops without ploughing the ground; they want rain without thunder and lightning; they want the ocean without the roar of its many waters. The struggle may be a moral one, or it may be a physical one, or it may be both. But it must be a struggle. Power concedes nothing without a demand. It never did and it never will.
>
> - Frederick Douglass

References

Douglass, Frederick. (1845) 1995. *Narrative of the Life of Frederick Douglass, an American Slave*. Boston, MA: The Anti-Slavery Office. Reprint, Mineola, NY: Dover Publications.

Douglass, Frederick. 1847–1874. Frederick Douglass Newspapers Collection, Library of Congress. https://www.loc.gov/collections/frederick-douglass-newspapers/about-this-collection.